The TAROT Workbook

The TAROT Workbook

A Step-by-Step Guide to Discovering the Wisdom of the Cards

NEVILL DRURY

NEW HOLLAND

Published in Australia in 2004 by
New Holland Publishers (Australia) Pty Ltd
Sydney • Auckland • London • Cape Town

Created and produced by Lansdowne Publishing Pty Ltd, CEO: Steven Morris,
email: sales@lanspub.com.au

Commissioned by Deborah Nixon
Text: Nevill Drury
Project Coordinator: Bettina Hodgson
Editor: Avril Janks
Designer: Robyn Latimer
Production Manager: Sally Stokes

10 9 8 7 6 5 4 3 2 1

National Library of Australia Cataloguing-in-Publication Data
Drury, Nevill, 1947- .
The tarot workbook : a step-by-step guide to discovering the wisdom of the cards.
Includes index.
ISBN 1 74110 134 4.
1. Tarot. I. Title.
133.32424

Set in Goudy and Stone Sans on QuarkXPress
Printed in China

The Tarot provides
us with a window to the soul.

CONTENTS

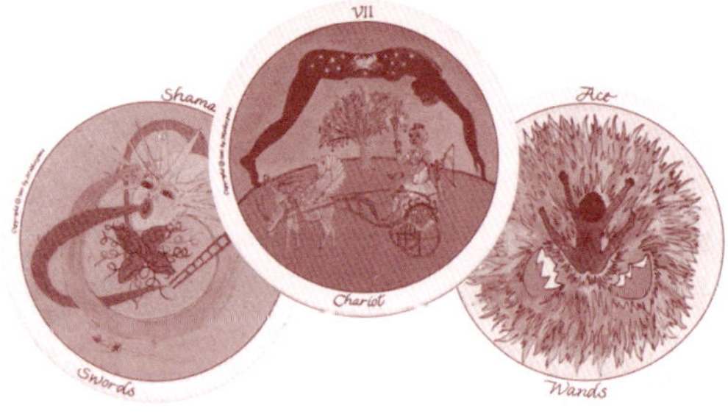

INTRODUCTION

The Tarot is one of the most fascinating of all Western mystical traditions and has been used for centuries for ***divination****, meditation, and visualization. While many people continue to equate the Tarot with fortune-telling, its scope is both broader and richer than this. Tarot card readings can certainly help us explore the forces driving our personal ***destiny***, but the Tarot can also provide doorways to the mythic aspects of our minds and souls. It can help us develop our psychic and spiritual potentials, and has an inspirational quality that has fascinated countless generations since it was first developed in Renaissance Italy in the early fifteenth century.

The Tarot Workbook is both a sourcebook and an interactive guide. It offers an overview of the many different aspects of the Tarot, and also presents a range of practical exercises and procedures to enrich your understanding of the cards and their meanings. Use the focus questions at the beginning of each chapter to guide your reading. Work at your own pace through the workbook exercises at the end of each section. Use them to guide your personal exploration of the Tarot.

OVERVIEW OF CONTENTS

The Tarot Workbook begins by offering advice on how to select the most useful introductory Tarot deck and on the value of keeping a journal of your own personal experiences and impressions. After providing a concise history of the Tarot, we then explore its structure. An analysis is included of the symbolism of numbers and the ancient concept of the four ***elements***—Fire, Water, Air, and Earth—which are mirrored in the four Tarot ***suits***—Wands, Cups, Swords, and Pentacles.

The Tarot pack consists of seventy-eight cards, divided into the twenty-two cards of the ***Major Arcana*** and the fifty-six cards of the ***Minor Arcana***. The Major Arcana—the so-called mythic cards of the deck—are very distinctive and are described here in detail. The

Terms described in the glossary (pages 186–187) are highlighted in **bold italic the first time they are used.*

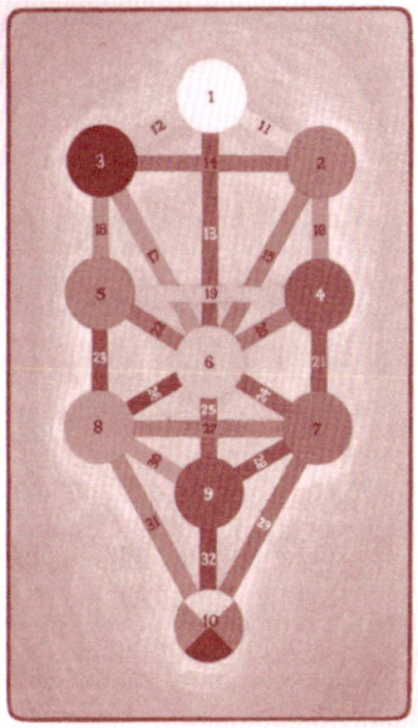

term "Arcana" (plural form of the Latin "arcanum") means profound mysteries or secrets known only to initiates. Collectively, the Major Arcana represent a mystical path of self-development that can take us to the highest sources of inspirational awareness. These cards are like pathways to the soul, which is why creative visualizations based on these cards are known as "***pathworkings***."

All of the Tarot cards are described in detail in this book, to guide you through the interpretation of their symbols and invite your reflection and response. Simple meditations on the Major Arcana are also provided.

Among the many Tarot spreads that have come down to us over the years, the Celtic Cross, the Gypsy Spread, the ***Three Aces*** Spread, and the ***Seven Card Spread*** are among the most evocative for modern-day readers. We explore them in this workbook. The necessary preliminaries for preparing a Tarot spread are explained at length, and we also explore simple "yes" or "no" readings and spreads intended for friends and lovers, including a variation on the Celtic Cross referred to here as "Tarot for Two."

The chapter on Tarot meditations and visualizations describes the connection between the Tarot and the mystical ***Kabbalah***—a connection now central to the Western esoteric tradition. This chapter includes a description of the spheres of the ***Tree of Life*** and the way in which the cards of the Major Arcana can be regarded as pathways linking these spheres.

TAKING THE TAROT FURTHER

Finally, we explore a number of other points that will enable you to take your study of the Tarot further: ethical issues, the need for effective communication during a reading, and the concepts of ***karma***, free will, ***fate***, and destiny. The Tarot remains one of the most popular of all the metaphysical wisdom traditions, and its appeal will surely extend far into the future. Our hope is that, in using *The Tarot Workbook* as part of your own exploration, you will enrich your personal understanding of this wonderful tradition.

CHAPTER ONE

THE HISTORY OF THE TAROT

Exploring myth, story, and fact about the Tarot and the Tarot deck: How did the Tarot originate? How is it linked with other mystical systems? How has the Tarot deck developed and changed over the centuries?

In the popular imagination, Tarot cards are associated primarily with divination and gypsy fortune-telling. Yet we know that medieval Tarot cards existed in Italy at least a century before the gypsies arrived in western Europe. The modern Tarot deck is descended from the Piedmontese Tarot and the Tarot of Marseilles, both of which were widely known in northern Italy and France by the beginning of the sixteenth century.

Even now, the specific origins of the Tarot—including the identity of the person or group of persons who designed the first deck and decided on the major symbolic references—remain inconclusive.

According to one account, the Tarot was created by a group of metaphysicians who met in Fez, Morocco, in 1200. Others claim that the Tarot originated in ancient Egypt, a view first put forward by eighteenth-century French theologian Antoine Court de Gebelin, author of one of the earliest books on the Tarot, *Le Monde Primitif*. One of Gebelin's followers, a wig-maker named Alliette, reversed his name to Etteilla and then published a book on the Tarot in 1783 in which he claimed that the Tarot had been created by seventeen magi, 171 years after the "Deluge" (the great flood documented in the Bible). Alliette created a deck of cards accompanied by a book, *Manière de tirer: Le Grand Etteilla où tarots Egyptiens*.

Despite the appeal of an ancient wisdom tradition in which priests and initiates pass down their secret magical knowledge to their followers, the views of Gebelin, Alliette, and others linking the Tarot to ancient Egypt, the magi, and Morocco are not widely accepted by Tarot historians today.

The earliest Tarot cards show robed monarchs, princes and princesses, castles, and armored knights, so it is likely that even though the images in the various Tarot decks sometimes include Egyptian symbols, the cards themselves are of medieval European origin.

So when exactly did the earliest Tarot cards first appear? We know from court records that in 1392 King Charles VI of France made a payment to a painter named Jacquemin Gringonneur for three packs of cards described as "gilded and colored, and ornamented with various devices, supplied to the King for his amusement." It is not clear, however, whether these were early Tarot cards or simply decorative playing cards. The Bibliothèque Nationale in Paris has in its collection seventeen cards, sixteen of them identifiable as Tarot cards. Originally thought to have been those created for Charles VI by Gringonneur, they are now regarded by scholars as Venetian in origin, and date from c. 1470. The Gringonneur cards themselves have never been found, so it is possible that Tarot cards did not exist as early as 1392.

Some historians and scholars believe that the Tarot cards were invented between 1410 and 1425 in northern Italy, and it is certainly the case that most of the decks that survive from fifteenth-century Italy reflect the fashion of the nobility of Milan and Ferrara from this period. The earliest known Tarot cards date back to 1442 and originated in the d'Este court of Ferrara. Interest in the Tarot then spread from Italy to France and on to other regions of Europe.

POPULAR DECKS

There are historical decks like the Tarot of Marseilles, the beautiful Visconti Tarot, the Florentine Ancient Minchiate deck, and the popular Swiss 1JJ (Junon) deck. Then there are the Tarot decks associated with the ***Hermetic Order of the Golden Dawn*** (an organization established in England in 1888), of which both A. E. Waite and Aleister Crowley were members. These decks include the classic ***Rider-Waite deck***, one of the most popular decks today, the Builders of the Adytum (B.O.T.A.) Tarot, the Golden Dawn Tarot, designed by MacGregor Mathers and his wife Moina Bergson, and the visionary Thoth pack, designed by Aleister Crowley and Lady Frieda Harris in the late 1930s and early 1940s.

Rider-Waite Deck

Egipcios Kier Tarot

Mythic Tarot

Golden Dawn

Motherpeace

Aleister Crowley Thoth

Native American Tarot

Tarot of Marseilles

Tarot of the Witches

THE RIDER-WAITE DECK

Arthur Edward Waite (1857–1942), chief among the Golden Dawn magicians, created the famous Rider-Waite Tarot deck together with Pamela Colman Smith. The name Rider-Waite refers to the Rider company in London, which first published the deck, and Waite's commentary on the cards in 1910. Waite believed that the four Tarot suits may have derived from the four sacred objects found in the medieval legends of the Holy Grail: the cup, the lance, the dish, and the sword.

THE B.O.T.A. DECK

Paul Foster Case (1884–1954) created the Builders of the Adytum (B.O.T.A) deck, which was illustrated by Jessie Burns Parke. Case claimed to be the American head of the Hermetic Order of the Golden Dawn and believed that he received "inner plane" teachings from the spiritual masters that guided this order in Britain. While we cannot prove or disprove his claim of spiritual guidance, the B.O.T.A. Tarot deck is remarkably similar to the Rider-Waite Tarot, both stylistically and in terms of its symbolic content.

A DIVERSITY OF MOTIFS

Some Tarot packs depict ancient Egyptian motifs. In the Rider-Waite and B.O.T.A. decks, the Wheel of Fortune depicts the jackal-headed god Hermanubis, the Chariot features black and white sphinxes, and the figure of the High Priestess is shown seated between Egyptian-style temple pillars. Other Tarot cards in these decks, however, such as the Hanged Man, the Devil, Death, Judgement (with its references to the Christian resurrection), and the Lovers (with its clear reference to Adam and Eve in the Garden of Eden), are more Judeo-Christian.

There are also alchemical and metaphysical references on many of the cards. Given the range of esoteric symbols that has infused the Tarot at different times through its history, it is quite possible that the medieval Tarot may have been disguising mystical ideas that in the Middle Ages would have been considered heretical. The suits on Tarot cards as we know them are Wands (Clubs are the equivalent in the modern-day pack of playing cards), Cups (Hearts), Swords (Spades), and Pentacles (Diamonds).

ARTISTIC STYLES OF THE TAROT

Artistic approaches to the Tarot have varied considerably over the years. The earliest designs were generally quite simple and were usually created through the use of wood blocks or delicate line engravings. A major exception to this is the exotic Visconti deck, whose richly embellished images have more in common with Renaissance paintings. Many eighteenth-century Tarot decks were stenciled and then crudely hand-colored, and continued the style established by the popular Tarot of Marseilles.

Today Tarot decks do not just depend on traditional imagery, but also draw on themes from many diverse sources. There have been all manner of experimental and fantasy decks, like the Celtic, Arthurian and Merlin decks, African, Native American, Mayan, Egyptian, and Aztec decks, the circular Motherpeace Tarot that celebrates Goddess spirituality, the highly stylized Aquarian deck designed by David Palladini, the Osho (or Bhagwan Rajneesh) Tarot, the Mythic Tarot, and the photomontage Voyager deck, among many others.

Among the most spectacular of the recent experimental decks is the visually striking Voyager Tarot, developed by American psychologist James Wanless. These cards consist entirely of composite images created through photomontage—each card is a distinctive artwork in its own right—but they bear almost no relation at all to the classic Tarot decks. The so-called Witches Tarot is humorous and stylized and was created to feature in one of the James Bond movies. Many of the other contemporary decks are simply unique, imaginative blends that tell far more about the personal tastes and interests of their creators than about the Tarot itself. Nevertheless, leaving aside their visual approach, most contemporary Tarot decks continue to employ the basic seventy-eight-card structure first established in Renaissance Italy.

LINKING THE TAROT AND THE KABBALAH

The Tarot, with its rich mystical and archetypal imagery, is a self-contained divinatory and meditative system. There is also some overlap with other spiritual traditions. For example, several modern decks include references to the Kabbalah, the sacred tradition of Jewish mysticism. The Kabbalistic symbol of the Tree of Life (see Chapter Three) can be used to extend and enhance our interpretation of the Tarot.

In the Middle Ages, the Tree of Life was used as a meditative framework for the exploration of mystical and visionary states of consciousness. The central texts of the Kabbalah were written down for the first time in the thirteenth century. In the nineteenth century, the French ceremonial magician and occultist Eliphas Levi (1810–75) first suggested combining the Major Arcana of the Tarot with the Tree of Life. Linking the Kabbalah and the Tarot, as Levi suggested, meant that the Tarot cards could then be used not only for divination, but also as pathways into the mystical realms of human consciousness.

THE TAROT AND WESTERN MAGIC

The Tarot has now become a central feature of the Western magical tradition, and this is due in large measure to the influence of Eliphas Levi. The Kabbalistic Tree of Life is regarded by magicians as a map of the soul. Levi believed that the Tarot cards incorporated a sacred occult alphabet. He linked the twenty-two paths that connect the ten spheres of the Kabbalistic Tree of Life with the twenty-two letters of the Hebrew alphabet, and, in turn, with the twenty-two cards of the Major Arcana. In his book *Dogme et Rituel de la Haute Magie*—published in English as *Transcendental Magic*—Levi described what he regarded as the source of the esoteric Tarot. He implied also that the Tarot was part of an heretical mystical tradition:

> *When the Sovereign Priesthood ceased in Israel, when all the oracles of the world became silent in presence of the Word which became Man, and speaking by the mouth of the most popular and gentle of sages, when the Ark was lost, the sanctuary profaned, and the Temple destroyed, the mysteries of the Ephod and Theraphim, no longer recorded on gold and precious stones, were written or rather figured by certain wise kabbalists first on ivory, parchment, on gilt and silvered leather, and afterward on simple cards, which were always objects of suspicion to the Official Church as containing a dangerous key to its mysteries.*

EXTENDING THE LINKS

Levi's concept of merging the Kabbalistic Tree of Life with the Major Arcana of the Tarot was developed by Gérard Encausse (1865–1916), a French physician who wrote under the name of Papus. In 1889 Papus published an influential work entitled *The Tarot of the Bohemians*, which included images created by Oswald Wirth, an artist. These images were modified to incorporate letters of the Hebrew alphabet, reinforcing the idea that the Tarot and the Jewish mystical tradition were symbolically interconnected. The idea of mapping the Major Arcana of the Tarot as a network of symbolic pathways upon the Tree of Life was then taken up by the ceremonial magicians of the Hermetic Order of the Golden Dawn. Today, the twenty-two cards of the Major Arcana are often linked specifically to the twenty-two letters of the Jewish alphabet.

USING THE TAROT CARDS FOR MEDITATION

The Tarot is best known for its many applications in fortune-telling. However, as it has been linked with the mystical system of the Kabbalah, it is important to consider the divinatory and meditative uses of the Tarot as well.

When used meditatively, the Tarot cards of the Major Arcana represent symbolic pathways to the Spirit—a journey through the mazes of the mind and soul. In the Western magical tradition, the Major Arcana have been mapped on the Kabbalistic Tree of Life to produce a framework of Western mystical consciousness. This system of mystical spheres and paths upon the Tree of Life (sometimes shown superimposed upon a human figure known as "Adam Kadmon") is comparable to the chakra system of Eastern yoga, where energy centers are also shown superimposed upon the body of a cross-legged meditating figure.

However, while the Kabbalah belongs to the Jewish spiritual tradition, the Tarot draws on other spiritual traditions as well for its imagery.

WORKBOOK EXERCISES

1. Research some of the earliest Tarot decks you can find. Compare the images in an early Tarot deck—like the Tarot of Marseilles, the beautiful Visconti Tarot, or the popular Swiss 1JJ (Junon) deck—with the Rider-Waite deck, the Crowley Thoth deck, or a contemporary deck like the Motherpeace Tarot.
   - What are some of the differences in images and symbols between the earliest decks and the most recent ones?
   - Which images in each deck resonate with you? And which images seem unappealing or inappropriate? Why do you think this is the case?
   - Reread your answers after you have explored the imagery of the Major Arcana and Minor Arcana in Chapters Four and Five.

2. Find out more about A. E. Waite and Pamela Colman Smith, creators of the Rider-Waite Tarot deck used to illustrate this book. Look up the Golden Dawn on the website www.hermeticgoldendawn.org for information on its members, and read the section on Pamela Colman Smith in Mary K. Greer's fascinating book, *Women of the Golden Dawn* (see Further Reading, page 184).

3. Find some modern Tarot decks that interest you. Which images resonate with you? Why do you think this is the case?

Rider-Waite Deck

Tarot of Marseilles

Golden Dawn

CHAPTER TWO

BEGINNING THE TAROT JOURNEY

Making a Tarot deck your own: How do I choose the best Tarot deck for me? How can I familiarize myself with the deck I have chosen? How can I connect with the cards?

CHOOSING YOUR DECK

In some ways the first step may seem the hardest. As your research in Chapter One has shown you, there are many Tarot decks available now. How can you make an informed choice—especially at the beginning?

The Rider-Waite deck is probably the best as a first choice, though the reasonably similar B.O.T.A. deck is a good alternative. Many of the introductory texts on the Tarot, such as those by Eden Gray, Rachel Pollack, Eileen Connolly, Robert Mueller, and A. E. Waite himself, include the images from the Rider-Waite deck, and their commentaries relate specifically to the themes and archetypal symbols featured in these cards.

The Rider-Waite and B.O.T.A. decks are sometimes referred to as "rectified" Tarot decks, meaning that they have reinterpreted earlier styles and themes as well as introducing additional esoteric concepts not found in the earlier decks. To this extent they serve to remind us that many details included in the Tarot are of comparatively recent origin, and that some of the symbols and images we are now so familiar with were not actually featured in the earliest Tarot decks at all.

The Rider-Waite deck is currently available in three sizes—large, medium, and small—the medium size being probably the most manageable. If you find that you wish to go beyond the rather traditional style of the Rider-Waite Tarot, you can always experiment with other decks later on.

PROTECTING YOUR PACK

Once you have chosen your Tarot deck, try to become as familiar with it as you can. Handle the cards frequently, shuffle them regularly, and build a rapport with the cards so you imbue them with your personal energy. Take time, too, to reflect on the individual cards, even before you have studied all their specific symbolic meanings in detail (see Chapters Four and Five for details about each card).

When you have finished using the cards on any given occasion, wrap them in a protective silk cloth or purse—gold, purple, mauve, and dark blue are ideal metaphysical colors for this purpose. Tarot silk bags and purses are often sold in New Age gift shops, or, if you are skilled at sewing, you may wish to make your own.

For storage, select an attractive, well-made wooden box. The box should be used only to store your Tarot cards, and for no other purpose. When you want to put your cards away, wrap them in their silk covering and then put them in the box in a secure place where they won't be disturbed. This way you will honor your Tarot cards and help to reinforce the feeling that they are special.

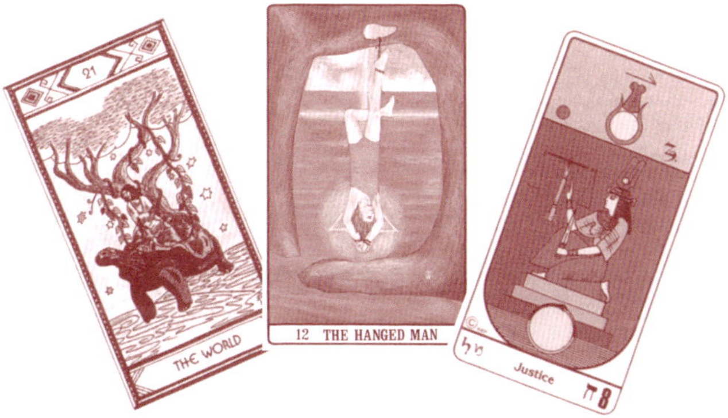

Explore the image styles of different packs when choosing your Tarot deck.

STAYING TRUE TO YOURSELF

It is important to remember that you will need to stay true to yourself when reading the Tarot cards. This will enable you to interpret the illuminating and often very profound themes the cards bear. The Tarot cards will serve as a trigger for your intuitive insights, and will enable you to develop your psychic and spiritual awareness. As you begin to explore the universal and archetypal themes of the Tarot, they will gradually be manifested to you through your own intuitive understanding.

If you are performing a reading for someone else, this is particularly important. The person seeking insight will be depending on you to maintain your integrity and your own sense of "inner knowing."

LEARNING TO RELAX

In order to access your powers of intuition, it is essential that you become centered on the task at hand. In the first instance, this means you will need to learn how to relax. The last thing you want to do is to project your own anxieties or tensions onto someone else during a Tarot reading!

There are many ways of relaxing, and you will need to find one that works for you. A simple and easy approach is described opposite. The important point to remember is that relaxation will provide you with a sense of openness and inner stillness that will allow you to center your awareness. Once you have achieved this sense of feeling focused and fully aware, you can concentrate on using your intuitive skills to explore what the Tarot cards are telling you.

KEEPING A TAROT JOURNAL

As part of your Tarot-reading routine, it is a good idea to keep a journal in which you can make daily listings. A ***Tarot journal*** is rather like a dream journal—a record of your psychic and intuitive impressions. You may receive intuitive impressions that you will want to think about later, or certain symbolic references may flash into your consciousness and will require further exploration at a later time.

SIMPLE RELAXATION

Sit comfortably on the floor or in a chair and loosen any items of clothing that are likely to cause distraction or discomfort.

Begin to relax different parts of your body progressively. You might like to begin by visualizing that your feet are becoming increasingly limp and relaxed; then imagine that your ankles and your calves have also relaxed in their turn.

Imagine now that your legs are completely relaxed, and that a soothing feeling of relaxation has entered your abdomen and is working its way into your upper body, stage by stage.

Now your chest is becoming completely relaxed and you are breathing deeply and without restriction.

Finally, relax your arms and allow the focus of your attention to remain solely in your head.

Now your focus should remain on awareness itself, for from this point onward your emphasis will be on summoning your powers of intuition—and tapping into those reserves of inner knowing that you will bring to your reading of the Tarot.

Note the effects of your meditation in your Tarot journal.

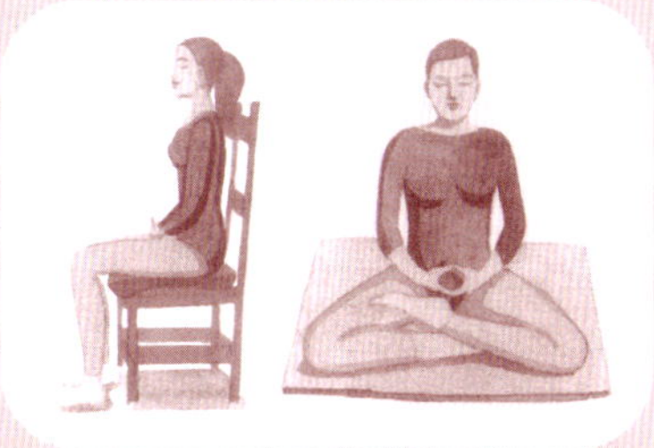

ENTRIES IN YOUR TAROT JOURNAL

At the top of your entry, record the date and time of your Tarot reading. Beneath this, list the particular Tarot deck used (e.g., Rider-Waite). Record the specific question that was the focus for the reading, and then list the cards in order of the spread, together with your interpretation of the cards (for more about spreads, see Chapters Six, Seven, and Eight). This will provide an excellent record for you, and also for the person for whom you are performing the reading. Naturally, such details should be kept confidential and stored in a safe place.

WORKBOOK EXERCISES

Each time you interact with your Tarot deck, refer to this checklist to ensure you are opening yourself up to the deepest possible insights in a Tarot reading:

1. Am I taking good care of the cards?
2. Am I taking good care of myself before a reading by relaxing?
3. Am I recording my intuitions and insights in such a way that I will be able to use them later?
4. Are the images I'm recording beginning to form a pattern? What could this be telling me? Write these details in your Tarot journal.
5. Does the Tarot deck I'm using feel "right" as a vehicle for tapping into my deeper levels of intuition and insight?
6. Am I developing a sense of spiritual rapport with any particular cards in the deck? If so, which ones? Write these details in your Tarot journal.

CHAPTER THREE

THE STRUCTURE OF THE TAROT

Discovering the symbolism of the Tarot cards: What do the numbers on the cards signify? How are the suits of the cards connected with the elements of Fire, Water, Earth, and Air? Why are the Court cards so important? How are the cards connected with the Kabbalistic Tree of Life?

THE SYMBOLISM OF NUMBERS

Numbers as symbols are an important feature of the Tarot, especially where the Minor Arcana are concerned. We could argue, in fact, that the Tarot consists substantially of a blend of archetypal images and numerical meanings. In each of the four suits of the Minor Arcana—Wands, Cups, Swords, and Pentacles—there are individual cards from Ace (One) through to Ten, and the implicit meaning of these cards is directly related to their numerical value.

Here is a summary of the symbolic significance of One through Ten, which will help you gain a clearer understanding of the nature of the Minor Arcana.

ONE

One is the beginning and is therefore associated with creative power, individuality, initiative, and unity. People with this ruling number are said to be independent and single-minded. One has its source in Spirit. It is the primary number from which all other numbers arise, the number that represents the One God and the true Self.

TWO

Two represents duality in all its forms—duplication, reflection, receptivity, alternation, antagonism (a continuous state of the nonresolution of opposites), and so on. It is associated with polar opposites like night and day, positive and negative, male and female, good and evil. Because, by its very nature, duality is not resolved, the number Two represents creativity unfulfilled, the creative interplay of opposites, represented by the Great Father and Great Mother of sacred traditions who give birth through their union.

THREE

This is a number associated with growth, expansion, ambition, and development. In its classic application a mother and father produce a child through their union, so symbolically Two begets Three. The Holy Trinity—Father, Son, and Holy Ghost—are the three different faces of the Divine in Christian tradition, and the number Three reflects the threefold nature we all share as human beings: body, mind, and spirit. In the Kabbalah, Three represents the Great Mother, the Great Holy Father, and the Source of Being. Three is the actual seed or offspring—in more general terms, it means specific results or the birth of something new.

FOUR

The number Four is symbolized by a square or cube and represents order, logic, classification, and measurement. It also represents the material universe and physical reality, because when the sacred Trinity gives rise to the universe, Three then becomes Four. For this reason, Four is also the number associated with hard work and practicality. This number reflects the foundation for the development of the new project or creation represented by Three. According to the Kabbalists, Four is the number of memory.

FIVE

Five has several meanings. It embodies the idea of many forces operating at once—perhaps at odds with each other—and for this reason is linked to change, uncertainty, activity, and freedom. It is also the number of versatility. It is associated with human aspiration as well, because the five-pointed star or pentagram represents the head, arms, and legs of a human being. When the pentagram points upward it is a symbol of positive, spiritual aspiration (white magic), and when it points downward it is a symbol of materialism and evil (black magic).

SIX

Six represents balance, harmony, symmetry, beauty, loyalty, and love. It is also the number associated with marriage and motherhood. Six is sometimes represented by the six-sided cube, a symbol of solidity. In the Jewish spiritual tradition, the Seal of Solomon (Star of David) is the six-pointed star consisting of two intersecting triangles, one triangle representing Spirit and the other material form, or Earth. It epitomizes the ideal of Heaven on Earth.

SEVEN

This number represents perfection, security, completeness, safety, victory, and rest (because God rested on the seventh day of Creation). It is also the mystic number symbolizing wisdom and spiritual self-development. There are seven notes on the musical scale, seven colors in the rainbow, and in traditional astrology there are seven planets. When we are in "seventh heaven," we are in a state of extreme happiness.

EIGHT

This number represents strength of character and individuality of purpose. Its emphasis is on sound intellectual judgement and the executive skills associated with personal mastery. It is associated with justice, health, balance, progress, and independent thought. On the Kabbalistic Tree of Life, the eighth sphere, Hod, is the center for rational intellect.

NINE

This is the culmination of all the numbers that have preceded it. Numerologically, Ten, which follows Nine, consists of 1 + 0, so Nine represents completion, attainment, and fulfillment.

TEN

This number represents the end of the cycle and a return to the beginning. It is therefore known as the number that symbolizes "perfection through completion." On the Kabbalistic Tree of Life, the tenth and final emanation from God is the physical world—the Kingdom of the Spirit. Numerologically, Ten (1 + 0) returns to unity.

The Ace through Ten within each of the four suits are sometimes known as the "pip" cards, and detailed descriptions of these cards are provided in Chapter Five.

THE FOUR ELEMENTS

The division of the world of creation into four elements—Fire, Water, Air, and Earth—is a metaphysical idea. It dates back to Empedocles and Aristotle in ancient Greece. It is also a key idea in Western astrology, magic, and alchemy. It is useful to consider the traditional attributes and qualities ascribed to each of the elements, for the elements relate to the Tarot cards, and knowing their attributes can assist us with interpreting the Tarot.

The four elements are linked to the four Tarot suits as follows:

△	**Fire**		Wands *
▽	**Water**		Cups
🜁	**Air**		Swords *
🜃	**Earth**		Pentacles or Disks

**Note: In some Tarot decks Wands are linked to Air and Swords to Fire, but the pairings listed above are the most common.*

ATTRIBUTES OF THE FOUR ELEMENTS

△ **Fire** *Masculine*: Vitality, strength, willpower, violence, passion, inspiration, optimism, enthusiasm, confidence, courage, aggression, domination, leadership

▽ **Water** *Feminine*: Receptivity, reflection, passivity, emotion, intuition, love, sensitivity, nourishment, sexuality, desire, psychic insight

🜁 **Air** *Masculine*: Intellect, reason, swiftness, flexibility, logic, discrimination, discernment, the exchange of ideas

🜃 **Earth** *Feminine*: Stability, fertility, physical life, work, achievement, loyalty, family, community, the material world

THE TAROT SUITS

We can also ascribe broad areas of human activity to each of the four Tarot suits:

Wands are associated with growth, energy, and personal enterprise, and with new ideas and creativity. Their counterpart in the modern deck of playing cards is the suit of Clubs.

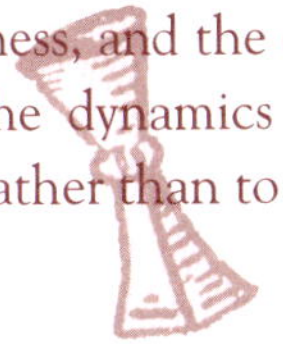

Cups symbolize love, happiness, and the emotions, and by extension are linked to fertility and beauty. In reflecting the dynamics of the psyche, Cups refer to the subconscious mind and natural instincts rather than to intellect or reason. Their modern-day equivalent is the suit of Hearts.

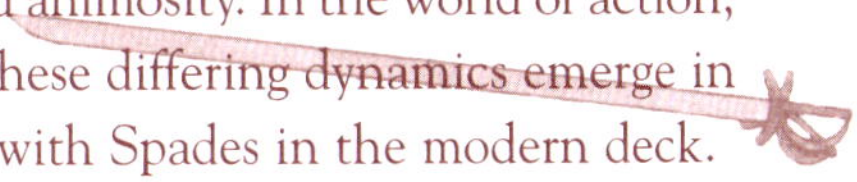

Swords represent aggression, force, ambition, struggle, and animosity. In the world of action, there can be both positive and negative dynamics, and these differing dynamics emerge in the different cards of the Minor Arcana. Swords equate with Spades in the modern deck.

Pentacles are associated with property and financial interests. In some decks the Pentacles, or Disks, are shown as coins. The coins represent the fruits of labor in everyday life. Pentacles correspond to Diamonds in the modern deck.

COMBINING THE ELEMENTS

As aware beings, we all reflect varying combinations of Fire, Water, Air, and Earth in physical makeup as well as in our temperaments and aspirations, our creative thoughts, and our everyday activities. Although Fire and Air are often said to be “positive” and Water and Earth “negative,” this is just a way of presenting symbolic opposites. Most of us are striving throughout our lives for a balance of all of these qualities.

How does each of the four elements reflect a different aspect of our individuality? Tarot writers Catherine Summers and Julian Vayne (see Further Reading, page 184) have suggested that our personal drive (Fire) is expressed through our intellect (Air), and supported by our intuition (Water). These forces then manifest in our physical body (Earth).

THE COURT CARDS

There are sixteen ***"Court" cards*** in the Tarot pack, four in each suit: King, Queen, Knight, and Page. In the modern-day suit, there are only three: Queen, King, and Jack. The Page, which could be male or female, has been omitted.

The Court cards reflect the qualities of Fire, Water, Air, and Earth. In all four suits:

- The King represents the ***Air*** aspect.
- The Queen represents the ***Water*** aspect.
- The Knight represents the ***Fire*** aspect.
- The Page represents the ***Earth*** aspect.

The allocation of Air to the King and Fire to the Knight may seem to be contradictory, but in medieval times the Knights were the aggressors and warriors, and the Kings more commonly the administrators or rulers. The medieval creators of the Tarot also recognized that each of the four elements has varying aspects: its most ethereal (represented by Air), its densest or most material (represented by Earth), its fluid qualities (represented by Water), and its dynamic properties (represented by Fire).

The Court cards combine the elements in different ways. For example:

King of Wands	=	***Air of Fire*** (the Fire card with the most ethereal aspects)
Queen of Wands	=	***Water of Fire***
Knight of Wands	=	***Fire of Fire***
Page of Wands	=	***Earth of Fire*** (the Fire card with the most material aspects)

The same applies to the other three suits, Cups, Swords, and Pentacles. All Kings represent the most ethereal aspect of the element. For example, the King of Pentacles represents Air of Earth.

MAKING ASSOCIATIONS

In general, when reviewing a Tarot spread, we can make the following associations:

- Kings with power
- Queens with support and creativity
- Knights with new projects
- Pages with new information

WORKBOOK EXERCISES

1. Compare the attributes for each suit with the attributes for the element associated with the suit (see pages 28–29):
   - The attributes for Fire and for Wands
   - The attributes for Water and for Cups
   - The attributes for Air and for Swords
   - The attributes for Earth and for Pentacles

   What insights into the suits do we gain from this comparison? How can this help us with interpreting the Tarot cards? Record your responses in your Tarot journal.

2. Now consider the elements in relation to yourself and ask these questions:
   - Which combination of the elements best describes who I am?
   - What aspects of Fire, Water, Air, or Earth manifest in my personality? If I had to choose, which element do I feel closest to?
   - Which element am I "strongest" in?
   - Which element or elements best represent aspects of my nature that I would like to develop?
   - When I consider the attributes associated with the four Tarot suits, which suit best symbolizes my deepest personal interests? Record your responses in your Tarot journal.

FINDING A SIGNIFICATOR

During a Tarot reading, it is generally said that the cards from Ace to Ten represent events that will unfold, and the Court cards represent the people to whom these events will happen. In order to provide readings with a more personal dimension, a Court card is selected from the deck by the ***reader***—the person performing the reading. This card then represents the person for whom the reading is given—the ***seeker***. The selected Court card, the card most like the person for whom the reading will be done, is known as the ***Significator***.

Prior to the actual laying of the spread, the reader has to decide into which category the seeker best fits. Here are the categories for selecting the Significator (the seeker who does not fit any of the descriptions entirely should choose the one that seems to fit most closely):

- ***Wands*** Fair hair, fair skin, blue eyes or red hair, fair skin, blue eyes
- ***Cups*** Light to medium brown hair and hazel eyes
- ***Swords*** Dark brown hair and brown eyes
- ***Pentacles*** White hair, fair skin, any color eyes or black hair, dark skin, dark eyes

The reader should extract the sixteen Court cards from the pack and lay them out in four rows (Kings, Queens, Knights, Pages) to help identify the Significator. The age of the seeker should also be taken into consideration:

- ***Kings*** represent older or middle-aged men
- ***Queens*** represent older or middle-aged women
- ***Knights*** represent young men
- ***Pages*** represent boys, young women, and children of either sex

Many Tarot readers believe it is fine for the seeker to have a say in choosing the Significator—after all, the choice is directly relevant to the seeker! For details of each Court card, see Chapter Five.

THE MYTHIC CARDS

The so-called mythic cards of the Tarot deck are the archetypal cards—the cards with the most complex and profound symbolic qualities, which incorporate universal themes. Because of their significance, they are referred to as the Major Arcana (see Chapter Four). And because they can be regarded as doorways to the soul, they are often used for meditation or visualization. We will explore this use of the Major Arcana in Chapter Nine. In the magical tradition, each of the cards of the Major Arcana is assigned:

- a *letter of the Hebrew alphabet*
- a *path* on the Kabbalistic Tree of Life
- a *ruling planet* or *ruling sign* in terms of astrology

The twenty-two cards of the Major Arcana are referred to as "Keys" and number from 0 to 21, commencing with the Fool and culminating with the World. The sequence is given on page 34.

THE MAJOR ARCANA

Key 0: The Fool (ruling planet: *Uranus*)
Key I: The Magician (ruling planet: *Mercury*)
Key II: The High Priestess (ruling planet: *Moon*)
Key III: The Empress (ruling planet: *Venus*)
Key IV: The Emperor (ruling sign: *Aries*)
Key V: The Hierophant (ruling sign: *Taurus*)
Key VI: The Lovers (ruling sign: *Gemini*)
Key VII: The Chariot (ruling sign: *Cancer*)
Key VIII: Strength (ruling sign: *Leo*)
Key IX: The Hermit (ruling sign: *Virgo*)
Key X: The Wheel of Fortune (ruling planet: *Jupiter*)
Key XI: Justice (ruling sign: *Libra*)
Key XII: The Hanged Man (ruling planet: *Neptune*)
Key XIII: Death (ruling sign: *Scorpio*)
Key XIV: Temperance (ruling sign: *Sagittarius*)
Key XV: The Devil (ruling sign: *Capricorn*)
Key XVI: The Tower (ruling planet: *Mars*)
Key XVII: The Star (ruling sign: *Aquarius*)
Key XVIII: The Moon (ruling sign: *Pisces*)
Key XIX: The Sun (ruling planet: *Sun*)
Key XX: Judgement (ruling planet: *Pluto*)
Key XXI: The World (ruling planet: *Saturn*)

Chapter Four provides a detailed description of each of these mythic cards.

THE TAROT AND ASTROLOGY

Most specialist writers on the Tarot and astrology agree that, as divinatory systems, each of these traditions has its own distinct origin and operates independently. Nevertheless, some links exist between the cards of the Major Arcana and the zodiac: each card has a ruling planet or zodiac sign. The planets and signs for the Major Arcana have been listed on the previous page.

The twelve signs of the zodiac are also linked with the four elements, as follows:

Fire	♈ Aries	♌ Leo	♐ Sagittarius
Water	♋ Cancer	♏ Scorpio	♓ Pisces
Air	♊ Gemini	♎ Libra	♒ Aquarius
Earth	♉ Taurus	♍ Virgo	♑ Capricorn

We can make a connection between the twelve Houses of the solar chart, the astrological ***ruler*** for each House, the corresponding Tarot card from the Major Arcana, and the assigned meaning in terms of divination. See pages 36–37 for a table listing these elements.

Note: *Combining astrology and the Major Arcana is a complex business, because there are twelve signs in the zodiac and seven traditional planets. Uranus, Neptune, and Pluto were unknown during the Renaissance, but have since been connected by modern Tarot writers with particular cards (Uranus with the Fool, Neptune with the Hanged Man, and Pluto with Judgement), to arrive at a total of 22 pairings. Without Uranus, Neptune, and Pluto, however, the fusion of the two systems would be incomplete—and it certainly would have been incomplete at the time the Tarot was first conceived. Interestingly, this modern blending of the Tarot and astrology may soon come under threat. Many contemporary astronomers now reject the status of Pluto as a true planet—it is only 1,440 miles in diameter—and approaches are currently being made to the International Astronomical Union to officially "delist" Pluto as a planet.*

SOLAR HOUSE	RULER	TAROT CARD	DIVINATORY MEANING
1st House [House of Self]	Aries	The Emperor	All beginnings, personality, physical appearance, outlook on life
2nd House [House of Money]	Taurus	The Hierophant	Financial matters, material possessions, tangible assets
3rd House [House of Communication]	Gemini	The Lovers	Communications, letters and writings, public relations, short journeys
4th House [House of Domestic Life]	Cancer	The Chariot	The first home environment, the mother, the imagination, the outcome of contests and litigation
5th House [House of Children]	Leo	Strength	Affairs of the heart, children, love affairs, adventures, speculations, exciting activities
6th House [House of Health and Work]	Virgo	The Hermit	Personal health, food, and hygiene, work and employees

SOLAR HOUSE	RULER	TAROT CARD	DIVINATORY MEANING
7th House [House of Marriage and Open Conflict]	Libra	Justice	Marriage, partnership, lawsuits, known enemies
8th House [House of Death]	Scorpio	Death	Legacies, deaths, taxes, a partner's money
9th House [House of Philosophy and Religion]	Sagittarius	Temperance	Law, philosophy, religion, ideals, higher education
10th House [House of Profession]	Capricorn	The Devil	Public life, social status, profession, honors, ambition, fame, the Father
11th House [House of Hopes and Wishes]	Aquarius	The Star	Friends, associates, groups, hopes, wishes, aspirations, public festivals
12th House [House of Bondage]	Pisces	The Moon	Personal limitations, secret desires, frustrated ambitions, unknown enemies, institutions that restrict or confine

THE TAROT AND THE KABBALAH

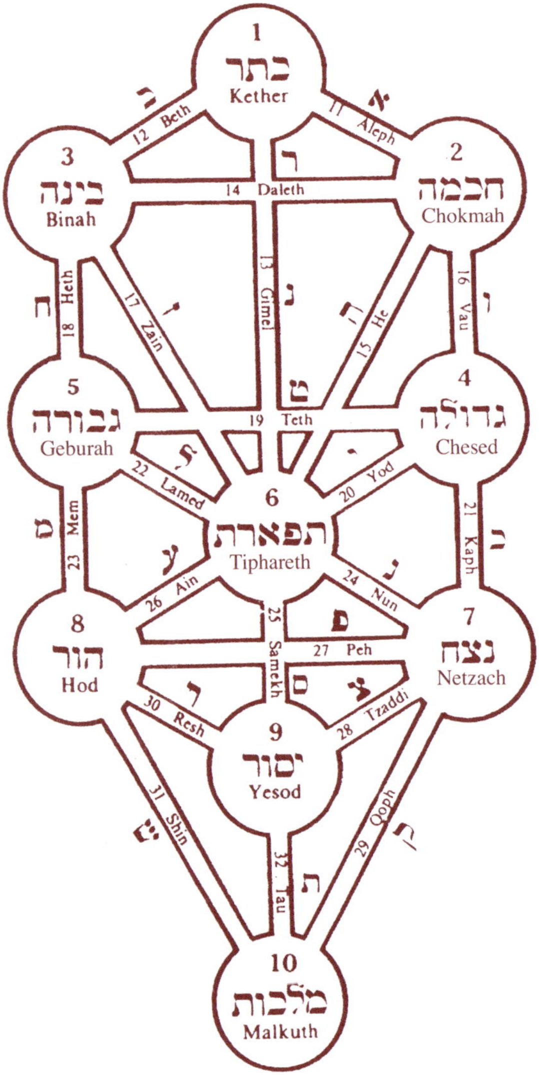

The Kabbalah is the name given to the sacred tradition of Jewish mysticism. The word "Kabbalah" itself translates as "from mouth to ear," and refers to a secret oral tradition. The Kabbalah is generally regarded as a mystical interpretation of the Torah, the first five books of the Old Testament, although the principal text of the Kabbalah—the *Zohar*—was not written down until the thirteenth century, when it was compiled by a Spanish mystic named Moses de Leon. Nevertheless, the Kabbalah is probably as ancient as the Old Testament Jewish tradition itself. Many scholars believe that the book of Genesis and the account of the Seven Days of Creation cannot be truly understood without an awareness of the spiritual themes of the Kabbalah, for it is in the Kabbalistic teachings that an effort is made to explain the symbolic aspects of the Creation process and the cosmological origins of the universe.

The Kabbalistic explanation of the Creation of the universe is based on a very profound theme—the idea of Spirit gradually becoming more manifest, producing a succession of different levels of mystical reality before finally giving rise to the physical world as we know it. According to the Kabbalah, before the world was formed the universe consisted basically of infinite sacred energy (known variously in the Kabbalah as En Sof, Ain Soph, or ***Ain Soph Aur***), and this sacred energy gradually acquired a more tangible outer form by manifesting through different levels of being. This process happened phase by phase—in the Kabbalah it is said that a bolt of lightning, representing the sacred life force, descended through ten different symbolic levels on the Tree of Life.

In the Kabbalah these ten levels on the Tree are known as ***sephiroth***, which we can think of as "spheres of consciousness." The first three sephiroth represent the Judaic Trinity and the next seven sephiroth represent the Seven Days of Creation. In the Kabbalah the ten levels of Creation are as follows:

Kether	*The Crown* or first point of Creation
Chokmah	*Wisdom* (the Father)
Binah	*Understanding* (the Mother)
Chesed	*Mercy*
Geburah	*Severity* or *Strength*
Tiphareth	*Beauty* or *Harmony* (the Son)
Netzach	*Victory*
Hod	*Splendor*
Yesod	*The Foundation*
Malkuth	*Kingdom* or *Earth* (the Daughter)

SYMBOLISM OF THE SEPHIROTH

The symbolic nature of each of these ten spheres of consciousness on the Tree of Life can be described as follows:

- ***Kether:*** This stage of consciousness represents Ultimate Reality—the first spark of Creation. Represents spiritual transcendence—the experience of Oneness.
- ***Chokmah:*** The sphere of wisdom, represented by the Great Father. He provides the spark of life that enters the womb of the Great Mother. The union of the Great Father and the Great Mother then gives rise to all of the images and forms of Creation.
- ***Binah:*** The Great Mother in all of her mythological aspects. In different world mythologies she is regarded as the Mother of Creation, or the Great Mother Goddess. Often she is the wife or lover of the ruler of the manifested universe.
- ***Chesed:*** The peaceful face of the ruler of the universe, and the qualities of divine mercy and majesty.
- ***Geburah:*** Represents severity and justice. The destructive energies of this sphere are intended as a purging, cleansing force. Considered positive rather than negative.
- ***Tiphareth:*** The midpoint between the world of everyday reality and the realm of ultimate spiritual transcendence on the journey toward mystical enlightenment. Symbolized by the Sun as a giver of life and light. Represents the theme of rebirth, or spiritual resurrection.
- ***Netzach:*** The sphere of intuition. Represents the arts, creativity, and the emotions. Also the sphere of love and spiritual passion.
- ***Hod:*** Intellect and rational thinking. Also represents the sense of order we perceive in the manifested universe.
- ***Yesod:*** Associated with the Moon, this sphere abounds in an ocean of astral imagery. Associated with dreams and the cycles of sexual fertility.
- ***Malkuth:*** Represents familiar everyday consciousness. Associated with the earth, crops, the immediate environment, and all living things.

PLACING THE TAROT ON THE TREE OF LIFE

As Eliphas Levi first suggested in the nineteenth century, the ten spheres of consciousness on the Kabbalistic Tree of Life—from Kether through to Malkuth—can be combined with the twenty-two Major Arcana of the Tarot, which then become symbolic pathways linking each of the spheres in turn. Because these pathways are milestones on the mystical journey back to God, we have to consider them in reverse order; in a mystical sense we now have to climb back up the Tree of Life to the spiritual source of Creation.

When the cards of the Major Arcana are mapped as mythic pathways on the Kabbalistic Tree of Life—from the lowest level to the highest—we arrive at a pattern like the one shown here.

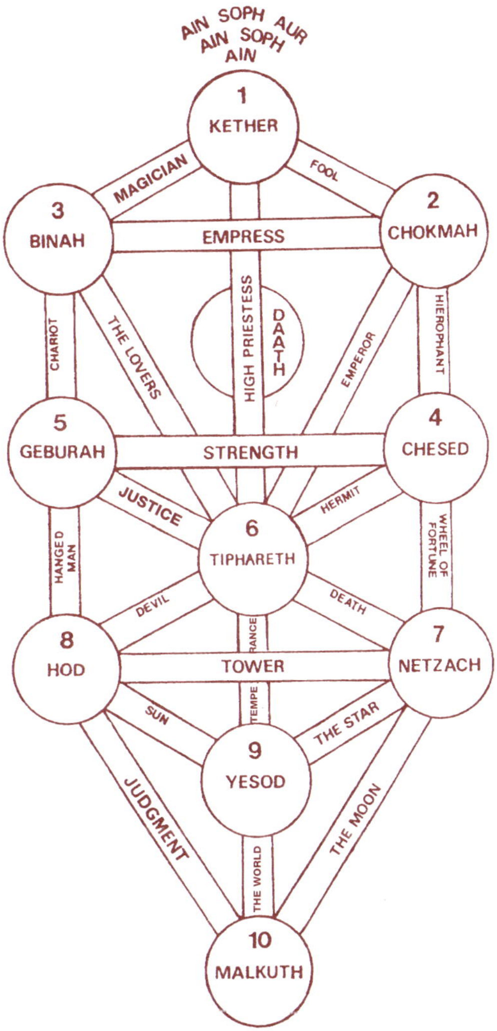

The World	Malkuth-Yesod
Judgement	Malkuth-Hod
The Moon	Malkuth-Netzach
The Sun	Yesod-Hod
The Star	Yesod-Netzach
The Tower	Hod-Netzach
The Devil	Hod-Tiphareth
Death	Netzach-Tiphareth
Temperance	Yesod-Tiphareth
The Hermit	Tiphareth-Chesed
Justice	Tiphareth-Geburah
The Hanged Man	Hod-Geburah
The Wheel of Fortune	Netzach-Chesed
Strength	Geburah-Chesed
The Chariot	Geburah-Binah
The Lovers	Tiphareth-Binah
The Hierophant	Chesed-Chokmah
The Emperor	Tiphareth-Chokmah
The Empress	Binah-Chokmah
The High Priestess	Tiphareth-Kether
The Magician	Binah-Kether
The Fool	Chokmah-Kether

Each card of the Major Arcana can be used as a meditative doorway: a door in the mind's eye through which one can pass to reach a higher level of understanding. Using the Major Arcana as meditative doorways on the Tree of Life involves what are known as "pathworkings." You will learn more about the complex concept of Tarot pathworkings in Chapter Nine.

WORKBOOK EXERCISES

1. Which number, from One to Ten, do you identify with intuitively? Once you have selected a number, go back and read the descriptions again at the beginning of this chapter. Does your choice reflect your true nature or personality?
2. Which of the four elements—Fire, Water, Air, and Earth—best describes your character or temperament? If you feel you are very much a combination, what combination describes you best?
3. Now correlate your choices with the correlations between the elements and the different signs of the zodiac listed on pages 36–37. Does your image of yourself correspond with your sun sign or your ascendant?
4. If you had to analyze yourself using the symbolism of the Court cards, how would you rate yourself from Air of Air through to Earth of Earth?
5. Once you have answered question 4, locate the specific Court card that actually represents the qualities you have nominated. Take a moment to visualize and meditate on this card. What feelings or impressions arise when you do this? Record them in your journal.
6. With regard to choosing the Significator for a Tarot reading, imagine that you are the seeker and that the reading is being done for you. Which card would you select as your Significator?
7. Look carefully at the Tarot paths on the Tree of Life.
   - What is the name of the Tarot card that represents the path linking Tiphareth and Chesed?
   - What is the name of the card that unites Binah and Chokmah?
   - Name the cards that define the "Middle Pillar"—the paths linking Malkuth, Yesod, Tiphareth, and Kether.
8. Take time, once again, to read through the descriptions of the sephiroth on page 40. Which sphere do you most identify with in terms of who you are now? Which sphere represents qualities you aspire to? What are these qualities? Write them in your journal.

CHAPTER FOUR

THE CARDS OF THE MAJOR ARCANA

The Major Arcana of the Tarot are the mythic, or archetypal, cards within the Tarot deck. This section provides a detailed description of each card and its meanings.

KEY O: THE FOOL

Hebrew Path: *Aleph* **Ruling Planet**: *Uranus*

DESCRIPTION This card occupies a unique position in the Tarot because no number is ascribed to it—its Key is Zero—and it is sometimes positioned at the beginning of the Major Arcana and sometimes at the end. The Fool represents both the beginning and the culmination of the mystical quest.

The Fool is the eternal youth, *puer aeternus*, and here we see him about to step off a cliff into the abyss below. In his left hand he carries a white rose representing spiritual desire, and in his right hand he carries a staff (or wand). Dangling from the end of the staff is a little bag or wallet containing the four elements—Fire, Water, Earth, and Air.

SPIRITUAL INTERPRETATION The Fool is a symbol for "he who knows nothing." On the path of Aleph the meditator draws near to the realm of mystical transcendence—No-Thing—that is unmanifest. This is a realm of true Mystery.

IN A TAROT SPREAD This card represents choice and receptivity. You will be offered a new opportunity or a new beginning. The Fool is embracing the adventure of life. So, too, will you. You are open to new suggestions and ideas and are not afraid of the unknown. Your attitude is one of serenity and trust. In terms of your personal relationships, this could be the beginning of something wonderful—the innocence of new love.

REVERSE MEANING You haven't given sufficient thought to the choices you are about to make. You are confused and could easily make the wrong decision.

SELF-DEVELOPMENT LESSON You are a child of the universe and you are open to all the new opportunities that life presents. Be prepared to "seize the day."

WORKBOOK EXERCISES

1. Spend a few minutes meditating or reflecting on the following words:

   My being is One with Spirit—without beginning or end.
   Within my heart I experience the innocence of youth and the
   ageless wisdom of infinite potential.
   I embrace the world, and I am open to what it offers me. May the
   Light of Life be my guide during my spiritual journey.

2. In your Tarot journal, list five important ways in which you are being sustained and inspired in your life at present (material, emotional, spiritual).
3. How willing are you to avail yourself of new opportunities as they arise? Write down three ways in which you have responded to new opportunities and challenges during the last twelve months.
4. Name five of your strongest fears. Now prepare a three-point strategy list for each of these five fears, outlining how you might deal with them.

KEY I: THE MAGICIAN

Hebrew Path: *Beth* **Ruling Planet**: *Mercury*

DESCRIPTION The Magician stands with his right hand held aloft, clutching his wand of power. His left hand points downward, indicating that he is transmitting sacred energy to the worlds below. Above his head is a horizontal symbol of infinity representing the Holy Spirit, and before him on a table—in effect his altar—are the symbols of the four elements. There is a cup (Water), a pentacle or disk (Earth), a wand (Fire), and a sword (Air). These are the elements of Creation. Red roses, representing desire and passion, form into a bower above his head and intermingle in the foreground with white lilies, symbolizing pure abstract thought. Around his waist the Magician wears the alchemical symbol of *ouroboros*—the snake of eternity devouring its own tail. In an archetypal sense, the Magician represents Divine Will.

SPIRITUAL INTERPRETATION The Magician gives rise to Creation. He raises one of his hands toward the realm of Spirit so he may draw down its sacred life force and transmit it to the many realms of manifestation below.

IN A TAROT SPREAD In drawing this card, you demonstrate that you have the power to act and make decisions. You are sensitive and intuitive in the way you make use of your power, and you are skilled in laying the basis for positive relationships. You are able to bridge the inner and outer worlds. This card is associated with the active will and also with sexual vitality. Drawing the Magician in a spread indicates that you bring an undoubted vitality and inspiration to your everyday life, and have a great ability to overcome conflict and push on to new heights. You are a true leader and an original thinker.

REVERSE MEANING You are using your power inappropriately or destructively. You are given to vain pursuits and are vulnerable to the influence of those who lie and deceive. Your projects are ill-considered and unlikely to succeed.

SELF-DEVELOPMENT LESSON True creativity means drawing strength from the inner realm of Spirit and manifesting this sacred force in the everyday world. In tapping into this sacred potential, you are inevitably developing greater self-knowledge, gathering renewed confidence to initiate new projects, and demonstrating heightened clarity of thought and insight in making your commitments.

WORKBOOK EXERCISES

1. Spend a few minutes meditating or reflecting on the following words:

   The sacred potentials available to me are infinite:
   I have the power to bring them forth into the world.
2. In your Tarot journal, list five qualities that provide you with a feeling of personal power and purpose. Do you have any attributes that you feel are sabotaging your present sense of personal power? What are they? Write down these answers in your journal.
3. In what ways can you bring a sense of Spirit through into your personal everyday life? List three ways in which you can draw on Spirit to enrich a) your family life, b) your friendships, c) your business activities.
4. Think of the various forces—both positive and negative—currently impacting your personal life. List five positive forces and then five negative ones. How do the lists compare? Is the overall thrust of your life positive or negative at present?
5. Draw up a five-point strategy list of affirmations that will help you bring your life into maximum positive focus. Write these in the present tense, e.g., "I undertake to..."

KEY II: THE HIGH PRIESTESS

Hebrew Path: *Gimel* **Ruling Planet**: *Moon*

DESCRIPTION The High Priestess sits on a throne located between two temple columns—the black column of Boaz, representing negative life force, and the white column of Jachin, symbolizing positive life force. These are the two pillars of King Solomon's Temple, and remind us of the historical connection between the Tarot, Freemasonry, and the Kabbalah. The High Priestess wears a silver crown showing the crescents of the waxing and waning moon, with the full orb in the center. A long cloak of blue and white flows down from her shoulders to the floor and seems then to become like a shimmering stream. On her breast the High Priestess wears a solar cross that unifies male and female energies, and across her lap rests the scroll of sacred memory inscribed with the word "Torah," meaning "law." In an archetypal sense, the High Priestess represents Divine Intuition.

SPIRITUAL INTERPRETATION On the Tree of Life, this Tarot path reaches to the very peak of Creation, the first sephirah: Kether, the Crown. Appropriately, the High Priestess herself has an element of untaintedness about her—she is unsullied and virginal. She has the potential for motherhood but has not yet brought to fruition the possibility of giving birth—of bringing essence through into form.

IN A TAROT SPREAD You are able to use your powers of intuition to receive higher spiritual inspiration. You may also find yourself tapping deeply into earlier memories, incidents from the past, and situations of conflict. There is an element of reserve and mystery in the High Priestess; she is guarding sacred knowledge. You may now recognize something that has been hidden. You have the feeling that you are being guided from within as she points to the ethereal level of existence.

REVERSE MEANING This indicates a tendency toward indulgence, superficiality, and conceit. There is little intuitive awareness here, only an appreciation of the external forces operating in everyday life. There are no secrets or subtleties in your world at present.

SELF-DEVELOPMENT LESSON You are opening yourself to your intuitive potential and heeding your higher spiritual guidance. Keep calm and tranquil, and trust your inner voice.

WORKBOOK EXERCISES

1. Spend a few minutes meditating or reflecting on the following words:

   Within my innermost being I honor the presence of the High Priestess.
   I open myself to the divine wisdom of the High Priestess and share her secrets and insights.
   I am a vessel for Divine Intuition.

2. In your Tarot journal, make a list of five ways in which you demonstrate an ability to act rationally. Now make a list of five ways in which you demonstrate an ability to follow your powers of intuition. Which list looks stronger to you? Do you depend too much on rational thought and neglect your capacity for intuition?
3. Think of a normal day in your life. On any given day, how much time do you put aside, if any, to open yourself to your powers of intuition? And how much time do you spend in silent reflection? Write down these details in your journal.
4. In response to the previous question, write down three ways in which you could allow more time for the voice of intuition to make itself heard in your everyday life and then make a commitment to yourself to put a five- or ten-minute period aside each day for silent reflection. Check a week later to see if you kept this commitment.

KEY III: THE EMPRESS

Hebrew Path: *Daleth* **Ruling Planet**: *Venus*

DESCRIPTION The Empress sits upon a cushioned throne in a rich, fertile garden. She wears a crown of twelve stars and a white robe decorated with flowers, and she holds a scepter indicating her power and authority in the manifested world. Her heart-shaped shield is inscribed with the astrological symbol of Venus. Behind her is a grove of cypress trees, also sacred to Venus, and in the foreground we see a field of wheat, sacred to Demeter and Hathor. The River of Life flows through her domain. We are reminded that every living creature that comes into the world is born of the Mother. The Empress provides us with the power to live and multiply, to give full expression to our dreams and our creative potential, and to appreciate the essential harmony and well-being associated with the deepest and most profound levels of existence.

SPIRITUAL INTERPRETATION The Empress is warm and beneficent. Laden with child, she is symbolically the Mother of All, since from her womb will flow all the potential images and forms capable of existence in the entire cosmos. Mythologically she is the Mother Goddess, and she represents the forces of Love and Nature on a universal scale.

IN A TAROT SPREAD This card signifies stability and harmony, and the prospect of growth and prosperity in all aspects of your life. It also represents fertility and the likely prospect of marriage. You are reaching a stage of considerable personal fulfillment, and your world and personal relationships are filled with joy and contentment. In a business context you are entering a phase associated with good opportunities and productive outcomes. You are happy with your life!

REVERSE MEANING You are engaged in unproductive activities and are not tapping into your full creative potential. You are dissipating your creative energies in a manner that may well produce disappointment or failure. Be wary of ostentation, poor judgement, and the powers of seduction. Postpone major business transactions and take the time to think more carefully about them.

SELF-DEVELOPMENT LESSON You have within you the potential to open your heart and mind to the powers of intuition and rational decision making. You can bring wisdom and understanding into your everyday life. This is a time for productive action.

WORKBOOK EXERCISES

1. Spend a few minutes meditating or reflecting on the following words:

   The world offers harmony, abundance, and endless opportunities if
   we are willing to accept this gift.
   My heart fills with love and contentment.
   I am a vessel for the healing powers of Nature.
   I give thanks for my life in the sacred garden of the Great Mother.

2. Name five ways in which your life is providing you with new opportunities—right now.
3. List five ways in which you respond to the challenge of your intellect. Now write down five ways (or, as many as possible) in which you listen to the voice of your heart. Which list looks stronger? List five ways in which you could strengthen your heart-feelings.
4. Have you found your true calling in the world? Write down three different options for careers or lifestyles that you could have opted for at an earlier time. Do you wish you had followed one of these earlier options? If so, is it too late to change?
5. List five current aspirations that you hold in relation to your life now.

KEY IV: THE EMPEROR

Hebrew Path: *Heh* **Ruling Sign**: *Aries*

DESCRIPTION The bearded Emperor sits facing us on his throne. He wears a crown and has an unquestionable sense of authority. He carries a Crux Ansata (Cross of Life) in his right hand and the globe of dominion in his left. Although he appears to be a monarch of peace, he wears medieval armor beneath his cloak, indicating that he has the potential for aggression. Rams' heads adorn his throne—the ram is a symbol of Mars, god of war. In classical mythology Mars and Venus were lovers, and in the Tarot the Empress and the Emperor are also lovers. Their union gives rise to all the manifested forms in the universe. The ruling sign associated with this card is Aries, a fire sign, and the mountains in the distance have a reddish tinge.

SPIRITUAL INTERPRETATION The Tarot path of the Emperor connects to Chokmah on the Tree of Life—the sacred sphere of consciousness representing the Great Father. As an archetypal figure, the Emperor embodies the qualities of divine mercy and extends his compassion to all his subjects. In relation to the manifested universe, he is the supreme active male principle, just as the Empress—Mother of the Universe—is the supreme female principle (the High Priestess and the Magician represent potentiality rather than active manifestation).

IN A TAROT READING This card signifies power and authority based on experience, and if you draw this card you clearly embody, or seek to embody, these qualities. You are a natural leader, you are ambitious, and you want to leave your mark on the world. You know how to arrange your own affairs, and you take responsibility for both your family and your business concerns. You may tend to be aggressive and stubborn, but you also have an innate wisdom that brings balance to your judgements and decision making.

REVERSE MEANING You are weak and lack authority. You show a tendency toward emotional immaturity and may be vulnerable to flattery. You do not take responsibility for your actions and display little ability to foresee future outcomes. You may also reveal an inclination toward brutality and petty despotism—hallmarks of an unjust ruler.

SELF-DEVELOPMENT LESSON True leadership requires a balanced outlook. This does not mean imposing your authority and demanding that others do everything your way: your leadership should draw on a broader, holistic vision and take heed of the needs of others.

WORKBOOK EXERCISES

1. Spend a few minutes meditating or reflecting on the following words:
   I open my inner being to honor the presence of high spiritual authority.
   I am filled with a sacred sense of balance and stability.
   I envision a world governed by tolerance, wisdom, and compassion.
2. In your Tarot journal, write down five ways in which you are able to demonstrate your powers of leadership and/or positive decision making.
3. Do you think of strength only in physical terms? Write down three ways you demonstrate emotional and mental strength. From what sources do you draw spiritual strength?
4. How tolerant and compassionate are you? Write down three ways in which you have recently demonstrated these qualities in everyday life. Rate your capacity for tolerance and compassion on a scale of one to ten.
5. How willing are you to forgive others? Think of a time in your life when you were called upon to forgive someone who had betrayed or disappointed you. How easily were you able to forgive this person? Rate your capacity for forgiveness on a scale of one to ten.

KEY V: THE HIEROPHANT

Hebrew Path: *Vau* **Ruling Sign**: *Taurus*

DESCRIPTION The Hierophant is a figure who reveals sacred things—he is a spiritual leader on earth. He has been described by Tarot authority Paul Foster Case as "a bridge-maker who provides a connecting link between outer experience and interior illumination."

The Hierophant sits on a throne between two stone pillars, just as the High Priestess sits between the pillars of Jachin and Boaz. He wears a triple-layered crown and holds a staff surmounted with three crossbars, indicating that he has dominion over the creative, formative, and physical worlds. Two monks kneel before him, their garments decorated with white lilies, representing pure abstract thought, and red roses, representing passion and desire. Between them are crossed keys—one of gold, representing the Sun (male), and the other of silver, representing the Moon (female).

SPIRITUAL INTERPRETATION The Hierophant embodies the enduring bond of wisdom and mercy. The inspiration of the Spirit manifests in the Hierophant as an archetypal expression of enlightened intuition. In theory, divine authority owes its inspirational origin to this realm of the Tree of Life. However, with the passage of time, worldly religious traditions often sink into dogma and conventionality. The card of the Hierophant reminds us that this need not be so, and that true spiritual insight transcends earthbound authority.

IN A TAROT SPREAD Because the Hierophant is a spiritual leader in the everyday world, there is an element of the conventional and the traditional in the way he goes about things.

If you draw this card, there is an indication that on one level you like to conform and to be held in high esteem by your peers. You are not especially receptive to change, and may have a tendency to be dogmatic and stubborn.

REVERSE MEANING You are open to new ideas and are not afraid to take risks. You are unorthodox in your beliefs. Take care, however, that you do not resort to superstition as a spiritual alternative.

SELF-DEVELOPMENT LESSON It is appropriate that we embrace spiritual truths and teachings that accord with our sacred inner knowing, are connected to our intuitive understanding, and owe their inspiration to a high spiritual source. Don't be afraid to be unconventional if your spiritual inclinations take you in a challenging new direction.

WORKBOOK EXERCISES

1. Spend a few minutes meditating or reflecting on the following words:

   I seek the highest spiritual truth for my guidance and inspiration.
   I seek to unify the inner world of spiritual illumination and the outer world of personal experience.
   I seek to walk in the light.
   I seek the source of the divine mystery that passeth human understanding.
2. How committed are you to religious/spiritual beliefs? Who do you trust spiritually? In your Tarot journal, write five sources of spiritual authority that have influenced you in your life.
3. If you have ever had a transformative spiritual or religious experience, write down the details in your journal. What did you learn from this experience? When did it take place? Have the effects been enduring and life changing?
4. Do you evaluate religious and spiritual teachings on their own merit, or are you more impressed by established traditions? Why? Write down five criteria you employ in order to evaluate spiritual "truth."

KEY VI: THE LOVERS

Hebrew Path: *Zain* **Ruling Sign**: *Gemini*

DESCRIPTION Adam and Eve stand naked in the Garden of Paradise. Behind Eve we see the Tree of the Knowledge of Good and Evil, and behind Adam a tree whose branches bear twelve flames representing the signs of the zodiac. Above them, with arms outstretched, is Raphael, archangel of Air—the element assigned to Gemini. Raphael is also linked to Mercury and represents the cosmic life breath. A mountain peak, representing the mystic quest and the abode of the gods, is visible in the distance.

SPIRITUAL INTERPRETATION On this path the Lovers or Twins (representing Gemini) stand naked in the innocence of Eden regained, and the Holy Guardian Angel towers above them, bestowing grace. Adam represents the male qualities of logic and rational intellect, and Eve the feminine qualities of intuition and emotional insight. As a result of the spiritual quest, these two polarities must eventually be united, for only then will harmony reign. The path of the Lovers flows upward from the sphere of Tiphareth (Haromy) on the Tree of Life, and shows the happy and enduring union of opposites.

IN A TAROT SPREAD This card is essentially about the attraction between two lovers, so on a human level it represents a very significant life choice. We all seek love, and we all experience temptation. At different times we are drawn on the one hand to vice and on the other to virtue. If you draw this card, you have to make an important decision or choice. This may be the beginning of a romantic partnership. Drawing the Lovers may also indicate that you are currently looking after another person, and the specific meaning will then be indicated by other cards in your spread. In a business context this card means your investments are protected.

REVERSE MEANING Infidelity and duplicity. You want the best of both worlds. Your loyalties are divided. You make the wrong choices. There are arguments over children or disputes with in-laws. Your social life is unstable.

SELF-DEVELOPMENT LESSON When love is guiding us, we embrace life's adventures in a positive frame of mind and we feel protected and supported in whatever we pursue. If we are united, we can work with our partner toward a joint goal—and this will in turn create happiness and harmony.

WORKBOOK EXERCISES

1. Spend a few minutes meditating or reflecting on the following words:
   I visualize my lover and offer loving support and care. Together we are One.
   I accept the inspirational guidance of my Holy Guardian Angel.
   I offer my innermost being unconditionally to Spirit.
2. Write down five ways in which you demonstrate loyalty to the person closest to you.
3. To what extent is your life inspired by love and companionship? Rate yourself on a scale of one to ten.
4. Do you care sufficiently for others, or are you inclined to become too caught up in personal issues? Rate your role as a "carer" on a scale of one to ten. If you scored five or less, draw up a five-point strategy plan for dedicating more of your life toward the care of others.
5. Do you ever open your heart completely to higher spiritual guidance? If you have been changed by such an experience, write down the details in your journal.

KEY VII: THE CHARIOT

Hebrew Path: *Cheth* **Ruling Sign**: *Cancer*

DESCRIPTION The heavenly ruler rides his chariot beneath a canopy of stars. His chariot is drawn by sphinxes. The white sphinx signifies mercy and the black the implementation of justice. The charioteer wears a crown surmounted by three golden diadems—eight-pointed stars—and crescent moons adorn his shoulders, reminding us that the Moon rules Cancer. The charioteer's hair is fair, like that of the Empress, and his belt is golden and decorated with the signs of the zodiac. He carries a scepter in his right hand as a symbol of his royal authority, and his chariot bears the motif of a winged globe, representing self-awareness and aspiration. The card of the Chariot represents the power of cosmic force.

SPIRITUAL INTERPRETATION The Chariot is a symbol of motion, and this Tarot card provides a possible symbolic connection with the Merkabah (chariot) tradition in Kabbalistic mysticism, which focused on the visionary journey of the soul from one heavenly palace to another. Here the chariot carries the heavenly ruler to the furthest reaches of his realm, while on the opposite side of the Tree of Life, in the sphere of Chesed, the ruler of the universe views his kingdom from the stationary vantage point of his heavenly throne.

IN A TAROT SPREAD This card signifies success or victory achieved through hard work and application. The charioteer embodies self-discipline and clear thinking. He can assess the situation, make key decisions, and then move on in a positive direction. If you draw this card in a spread, the chances are that you will overcome ill health and any other obstacles that currently impede your progress, and that you will be successful with any financial transactions in which you are currently engaged.

REVERSE MEANING You are using your talents and energies in the wrong way. Your life lacks balance and self-control. You are acting unethically or irresponsibly. You may suffer ill health.

SELF-DEVELOPMENT LESSON Genuine progress requires self-control, clear vision, and a willingness to act. Life is both a challenge and an adventure. Balance your inner inspirational wisdom with your worldly experience, and your life's journey will be fruitful and worthwhile.

WORKBOOK EXERCISES

1. Spend a few minutes meditating or reflecting on the following words:

   I am a vehicle for a higher spiritual purpose.
   My horizons know no boundary.
   I honor the inner and outer realms of knowledge and understanding.
   I go forward on life's journey with positive intent.

2. How decisive are you? In your Tarot journal, write down three examples of decisive action in the past month that have led to positive outcomes.
3. Do you ever sabotage the need to take decisive action? How have you done this? Is the problem likely to recur? If you think it is, prepare a list of five positive affirmations that will help you to become more decisive. Write these affirmations in present tense.
4. How selfish are you? Write down three ways in which you indulged yourself in the past month. Now write down three or more ways in which you helped someone else during the past month. Compare your lists. Rate yourself on a scale of one to ten.
5. If you rated yourself five or less in the previous question, draw up a five-point strategy list of ways in which you can help other people and put their needs ahead of your own.

KEY VIII: STRENGTH

Hebrew Path: *Teth* **Ruling Sign**: *Leo*

DESCRIPTION A woman wearing flowers in her hair, and also around her waist, is taming a lion and placing a garland around its neck. The woman has fair golden hair, like the Empress, and wears a white gown, symbolic of spiritual purity. In conquering the lion—an alchemical symbol of Fire—she is showing us that our higher spiritual nature can overcome worldly desires.

SPIRITUAL INTERPRETATION This Tarot path is positioned horizontally across the Tree of Life and occupies an equivalent position to the Tower, but higher up. Whereas the Tower separates the ego-based personality from the true spiritual self, Strength represents the gulf between individuality and universality. The fact that the woman can so effortlessly tame the lion demonstrates the triumph of spiritual intuition over brute strength. This symbolizes mastery over any vestiges of the "animal soul" that remain in the individual consciousness.

IN A TAROT SPREAD This card teaches us not only that courage and perseverance will help us overcome our problems, but also that the powers of love and intuition are stronger and more enduring than hatred, brute force, and antagonism. Drawing this card signifies that you have overcome any fears you may have had in the past, and that you are now mustering your resources and energies for the next phase in your life's journey. It may also indicate, however, that while you have achieved great things through your perseverance and determination in the past, in the future you will succeed just as effectively, and at less personal cost, by bringing more love and consideration into your everyday affairs.

REVERSE MEANING You are able to demonstrate effective mastery in worldly and material matters, but you lack love and intuition in your dealings with others. You have not been handling things effectively, and your personal and emotional affairs are in a state of conflict. You have lost sight of the spiritual side of life.

SELF-DEVELOPMENT LESSON Love conquers hate. You have the potential to transform your physical, mental, and sexual energies into a spiritual force that will take you into new realms of intuitive awareness.

WORKBOOK EXERCISES

1. Spend a few minutes meditating or reflecting on the following words:
   I open myself to guidance from my higher spiritual self.
   I experience the triumph of love and compassion over negativity, aggression, and blame.
   I seek to balance the forces of spiritual insight and material attainment in my everyday life.
2. In your Tarot journal, write down three dominant forces that exercise a strong influence in your life. Are you in control of these forces or do they control you?
3. How driven are you by worldly ambition and by a desire for material gain? Write down a ten-point "ambitions" list covering all your main interests and aspirations. Do your ambitions mostly benefit only yourself, or do they have the potential to help others as well? Rate this on a scale of one to ten.
4. Rate yourself as materialistic or spiritual on a scale of one to ten. Are you happy with this, or do you have plans for change? Write down these plans in your journal (you can look at them again in a year's time to see what transpired).
5. What are your personal sources of inner strength? Have they ever been put to the test? What happened, and what was the outcome? Write down these details in your journal.

KEY IX: THE HERMIT

Hebrew Path: *Yod* **Ruling Sign**: *Virgo*

DESCRIPTION The bearded hermit, clad in a hood and a heavy gray cloak, stands alone on a mountain peak. In his left hand he holds a long and sturdy staff, and in his right a lantern to help him find his way through the darkness on the perilous rocky track. The Hermit is wise and all-knowing and is sometimes referred to as the Ancient of Days. While he may seem to be alone, he is really a guide for those spiritual travelers who are climbing the mystic mountain a little lower down the slope. His lantern provides the beacon of inspiration, banishing the dark forces of ignorance and negativity, and guiding them ever closer to their goal of union with the Divine.

SPIRITUAL INTERPRETATION The Hermit wends his way up the magic mountain, but his final goal of mystical union with the Oneness of the Godhead is firmly in his mind, and the lamp he holds aloft illumines the pathway for all spiritual seekers who follow in his footsteps.

IN A TAROT SPREAD This card is associated with solitude and contemplation—the spiritual journey is all-important in your life at this time. Drawing this card signifies that you may soon meet someone who will become your spiritual guide and who can show you new possibilities for growth and heightened awareness. It also signifies a willingness on your part to accept help when it is offered. Be patient, however, for the spiritual path is long and arduous and there are no quick answers or easy solutions. Use your powers of discrimination and discernment in moving forward, and trust the light and wisdom of your own inner guidance.

REVERSE MEANING You reject the guidance and good counsel offered by others. You seem unwilling to avail yourself of new experiences. You offer too much resistance or create obstacles for yourself along the way. Your pride and ego are getting in the way of your spiritual understanding.

SELF-DEVELOPMENT LESSON The spiritual path that takes us through the darkness of our ignorance and leads us toward the light is narrow, and not without its challenges. However, if you open your heart and mind to spiritual guidance when it is presented to you, you will overcome the obstacles that appear before you and eventually reach your goal.

WORKBOOK EXERCISES

1. Spend a few minutes meditating or reflecting on the following words:

   Ask and it shall be given; seek and ye shall find.
   From within the darkness of my deepest fears I feel a guiding light gathering strength and filling me with a feeling of peace and understanding.
   I welcome the lamp of truth and open my heart to higher spiritual guidance.
2. In your Tarot journal, list the five biggest disappointments of your life. How did you respond to these disappointments? Would you respond differently today?
3. Do you allow unnecessary obstacles to block your progress? Write down three recent occasions when this happened. Reflect on these instances and prepare a five-point strategy list for dealing with self-sabotage. Write these points as positive affirmations, e.g., " I undertake to..."
4. Do you trust the leadership skills of others? Write down three instances where you have benefited from someone else's leadership.
5. How would you define your "spiritual path"? Write down your response in your journal.

KEY X: THE WHEEL OF FORTUNE

Hebrew Path: *Kaph* **Ruling Planet**: *Jupiter*

DESCRIPTION Adapted from the Wheel of Ezekiel, the Tarot card known as the Wheel of Fortune is dominated by the wheel motif in the center. Located at the four corners of the card are the four creatures mentioned in Ezekiel 1:10 and Revelations 4:7. They represent the four fixed signs of the zodiac and are as follows: the bull (Taurus), the lion (Leo), the eagle (Scorpio), and the human (Aquarius). The rim of the Wheel has the letters ROTA (TARO) inscribed upon it, interspersed with the Hebrew letters JHVH, which make up the sacred name of God. The Wheel itself has eight spokes. The three uppermost spokes have, on their tips, and reading from left to right, the alchemical symbols for salt, mercury, and sulfur, while the lowest tip has the astrological symbol for Aquarius. Seated on top of the Wheel is the sphinx, representing the true spiritual self, while on the lower right-hand side we see Hermanubis (Hermes-Anubis), the Greco-Egyptian deity who represents the evolution of human consciousness.

SPIRITUAL INTERPRETATION The message of this card is essentially that, while the cycles of change are part of everyday life, the essence of spiritual reality is timeless and unchanging. This Tarot card symbolizes the forces of fate and destiny.

IN A TAROT SPREAD You are assured of success. The position and nature of the other cards in your spread may provide an indication of the sort of success you can expect.

Drawing this card signifies that the laws of destiny favor you at this time and your relationships at home and in business will prosper.

REVERSE MEANING You are out of luck for the moment. This is a time to summon your reserves of strength and courage. You may be experiencing a setback at present, but do persist, because in due course you will reap what you sow. Good times lie ahead.

SELF-DEVELOPMENT LESSON It may be a cliché, but it also happens to be true: The only thing certain in life is change. We all experience the lows and highs of everyday existence, but finally the spiral of change tends upward as we grow in spiritual awareness.

WORKBOOK EXERCISES

1. Spend a few minutes meditating or reflecting on the following words:

   What is my form? What is my essence?
   I focus on my spiritual center—my true and unchanging self.
   I experience constancy and eternal peace within my inner being,
   amid the cycles of endless external change.
2. How willing are you to embrace change and "go with the flow"? If "likes complete predictability" is zero and "embraces all forms of change" is ten, rate yourself on a scale of one to ten.
3. In relation to the previous question, how happy are you with this evaluation? If you would like to change your approach in some way, draw up a five-point strategy list of positive affirmations that are, in effect, promises to yourself to embrace change more readily.
4. Do you believe you are master of your own destiny or subject to circumstances beyond your control? Write down your response in your journal.
5. Read the section on fate, karma, and destiny in Chapter Ten and record your personal views about these topics in your journal.

KEY XI: JUSTICE

Hebrew Path: *Lamed* **Ruling Sign**: *Libra*

DESCRIPTION The female figure of Justice sits on her throne between two pillars. She wears a crown whose main features include three turrets and a square jewel, and she holds the golden scales of justice in her left hand. In her right hand she holds an upright sword. This figure of Justice does not wear a blindfold over her eyes, but conveys an impression of strict impartiality and authority nevertheless. She has a green cape—the color of Venus—and a red robe—the color attributed to Mars. Ruled by Venus, this path leads to the sphere of her lover Mars on the Tree of Life, and is appropriately designated by the figure of Venus holding scales and the sword of justice.

SPIRITUAL INTERPRETATION In Eastern mysticism the Tarot path of Justice would be considered a path of karma—a path where the individual encounters the consequences of his or her actions. Justice demands balance, adjustment, and total impartiality. On this path, the meditator begins to discover the nature of the true, inner self by overcoming the illusory aspects of outer appearances.

IN A TAROT SPREAD This card represents balance, fairness, and impartial judgement. Drawing this card signifies that in your domestic or business life justice will prevail. This may well portend a new cycle of equilibrium and harmony at home or at work. You will receive what is due to you. In terms of your personal relationships, you may have to assess whether you are being fair to your partner, both emotionally and sexually, because you would surely expect the same sort of consideration in return.

REVERSE MEANING You are suffering injustice or loss. You are enmeshed in legal complications. You are betrayed by an act of prejudice. Someone you know feels inadequate but is unable to change the present course of events.

SELF-DEVELOPMENT LESSON In response to the universal law of cause and effect, we all have to bear the full responsibility for our thoughts and actions. Sooner or later, you will feel the full thrust of their consequences—for better or for worse.

WORKBOOK EXERCISES

1. Spend a few minutes meditating or reflecting on the following words:

   With eyes closed, I look inward. Do I like what I see?
   I seek forgiveness from those whom I have harmed.
   I seek harmony and balance in my relations with others.
   I am responsible for all my thoughts and actions and fully accept their consequences, now and in the future.
2. What is more important to you: your business activities or your personal relationships? In your Tarot journal, write down the ten activities in your daily life that you value most.
3. Recall three occasions when you treated someone else unfairly in a business transaction or executive decision. Write down the details and then also write down how you would respond in a similar situation if it happened again.
4. Write down the five leading criteria that you associate with ethical behavior.
5. Do you respect the rights of others—especially those who hold views that differ from your own? Rate yourself on a scale of one to ten. If you scored five or less, draw up a five-point strategy plan detailing ways in which you can become more tolerant of other people's viewpoints.

KEY XII: THE HANGED MAN

Hebrew Path: *Mem* **Ruling Planet**: *Neptune*

DESCRIPTION A young man whose head is glowing with radiant light hangs upside down, suspended from a T-shaped wooden cross. Leaves are sprouting from the cross, indicating that it is vibrant and alive—a symbol of cosmic life. One of the man's legs is bent behind the other, so his legs are also in the formation of a cross. The garment he is wearing is blue, symbolic of Water, while his legs are red, representative of Fire—there is a clear presence of complementary elements and this, like the number Four and the symbol of the cross, signifies balance. The figure of the Hanged Man personifies the act of surrendering to higher wisdom or, as Paul Foster Case has expressed it, "the submission of the personal consciousness to the direction of the Universal Mind."

SPIRITUAL INTERPRETATION This Tarot path, like that of Justice, leads to Geburah, the sphere of action. The Hanged Man swings by his foot, symbolizing sacrifice, but because of his inverted position he can also be compared to a reflection in water, the element ascribed to this path. The head of the Hanged Man is all aglow—he is reflecting inspirational light through to the lower levels of the Tree of Life.

IN A TAROT SPREAD The Hanged Man is a vehicle for the light of higher spiritual wisdom, so drawing this card signifies that you have embarked upon, or will soon undertake, a journey of spiritual growth. This may well indicate that you are about to leave your old self behind, abandoning your more materialistic and worldly concerns in favor of a path toward spiritual enlightenment. This card is also about acceptance and the capacity to remain open to new ideas.

REVERSE MEANING You are neglecting your spiritual potential and have become more preoccupied with your worldly self. You have closed your heart and mind to spiritual guidance. You are vulnerable to the influence of others who do not have your interests at heart and may deceive you. You should act cautiously and avoid making hasty decisions. You may also find it helpful to question the values and beliefs you currently hold.

SELF-DEVELOPMENT LESSON We all have the potential to become vehicles for the light and to learn to reflect a higher spiritual wisdom in our everyday lives. In doing this we will learn to forgo the desires and preoccupations of the worldly self and surrender to the power of cosmic guidance.

WORKBOOK EXERCISES

1. Spend a few minutes meditating or reflecting on the following words:

   I surrender to the guidance of the Spirit.
   I am a vehicle for the light.
   Spiritual radiance filters in all directions through the crystal-clear Ocean of Being.
2. In your Tarot journal, write down your five leading criteria for material success. Now write down your five leading criteria for spiritual well-being and fulfillment. Which list looks stronger to you?
3. Based on your previous response, write down your response to the following question: "Does my life have a spiritual purpose or do I live mostly just from day to day?" If you have any plans for change in the year ahead, write down these plans in your journal.
4. Define your spiritual purpose in life, and write it down in your journal.
5. What are your three greatest sources of inspiration?

KEY XIII: DEATH

Hebrew Path: *Nun* **Ruling Sign**: *Scorpio*

DESCRIPTION A skeleton clad in a suit of armor is shown riding a white horse and holding aloft a banner of a five-petaled rose—a symbol of Mars, the Roman god of war. The body of a slain king lies on the ground, and nearby a child offers a small bouquet of flowers. A young maiden kneels on the ground, her head cast to one side in a gesture of submission. A bishop is also shown, standing beside her and clasping his hands together as he submits to the rule and dominance of the figure of Death. The bishop wears a fish-head miter, representing the religious traditions of the Age of Pisces (the Christian era). The designer apparently wished to portray the death of the Age of Pisces and hint at the new spirituality that would emerge in its place. The rising sun, representing spiritual rebirth and renewal, is clearly visible on the horizon.

SPIRITUAL INTERPRETATION The Tarot card of Death indicates the limited nature of the ego-bound personality. In the mystical traditions, death heralds new life, and here, in the distance beyond the skeleton-figure on the horse, we see the sun rising over the horizon. On the Tree of Life the path of Death leads to Tiphareth, the sphere of spiritual awakening. Despite its confronting imagery, the path through Death leads inevitably toward spiritual rebirth.

IN A TAROT SPREAD This card represents change, transition, rebirth, and renewal. Drawing this card signifies that you are about to experience a period of change and you must now try to leave the past behind you. You are now called to face the future with renewed hope and confidence, in the knowledge that the change you will experience will be for the best.

REVERSE MEANING You are lapsing into temporary stagnation or inertia. You feel depressed and are in need of new ideas and motivation. This card may also indicate the death of a prominent person or impending disaster.

SELF-DEVELOPMENT LESSON To develop spiritually, we have to leave our material selves behind and be reborn in the light. Death is never final—it is a state of transition.

WORKBOOK EXERCISES

1. Spend a few minutes meditating or reflecting on the following words:
   What do I fear most about death?
   Can I leave my old, outmoded ways of being behind, and now move forward?
   Am I now able to face the figure of Death and not fear him?
2. In your Tarot journal, list five qualities that you associate with material success and five qualities that you associate with spiritual progress and development. Which of these qualities are more important to you?
3. On a scale of one to ten, rate your personal commitment to the process of spiritual awakening and transformation.
4. Have you ever had a near-death experience (NDE)? How have you been changed by it? If you haven't had an NDE yourself, research the literature and explore the way in which people who have these experiences change their spiritual focus following a close encounter with death.
5. If something in you had to die so that another part of you could progress to the next stage of life, what aspect of yourself would you discard? Write down your answer in your journal.

KEY XIV: TEMPERANCE

Hebrew Path: *Samekh* **Ruling Sign**: *Sagittarius*

DESCRIPTION The archangel of Fire, Michael, stands astride a river of light and pours the waters of Life from a Sun-vessel into a Moon-vessel. This constitutes a tempering, or union of opposites—a blending of solar and lunar energies. A halo of light surrounds Michael's head and the triangle of Spirit is clearly visible on his breast. One of Michael's feet rests in the stream—representing the waters of spiritual consciousness—while the other rests on the earth, symbolic of physical manifestation. In the distance the rising sun of spiritual rebirth dawns between two mountain peaks.

SPIRITUAL INTERPRETATION This card represents the path of direct mystical ascent to a state of spiritual illumination. Michael is the archangel of Fire, and this element is closely linked to Tiphareth, home of the spiritual Sun. Sagittarius, also a Fire sign, rules this path on the Tree of Life. In Greek mythology, iris flowers were sacred to Iris, goddess of the rainbow and messenger of the gods. The rainbow is also a symbol of God's promise to humanity. The act of tempering, or adapting, one thing to another is essentially about creating a state of balance and harmony. On the Tree of Life, Tiphareth is the sphere of spiritual harmony.

IN A TAROT SPREAD This card represents balance, coordination, and the ability to live and work in harmony with others. Drawing this card suggests you embody these qualities. Your attitude to life reflects a strong sense of personal integrity, and you are able to harness both your emotional and intellectual qualities in your dealings with other people. Your personal and business affairs are stable and balanced, and you feel secure and happy with your life. It is important that you retain this sense of security and stability, however. Be patient as you explore new possibilities and build for the future.

REVERSE MEANING Your business and personal affairs are competing with each other. You feel emotionally unstable. Your judgement is failing you at present. Your creative energies are being dissipated. Pause and reevaluate the key aspects of your life before proceeding to something new.

SELF-DEVELOPMENT LESSON True harmony and integrity become possible when you learn to balance the material and spiritual aspects of your life.

WORKBOOK EXERCISES

1. Spend a few minutes meditating or reflecting on the following words:

   I offer myself as a vessel for peace, balance, and stability.

   I seek a balance of spiritual awakening and worldly understanding in my everyday life.

   I honor both Sun and Moon as companions within my heart.
2. In situations of conflict, how willing and able are you to see the other person's point of view? Rate yourself on a scale of one to ten.
3. How harmonious are your present relations with friends and family, and how important are these relationships to you? Write down your responses.
4. How would you define a state of true inner balance? Write down your definition in your Tarot journal.
5. List five qualities that you associate with personal integrity.

KEY XV: THE DEVIL

Hebrew Path: *Ayin* **Ruling Sign:** *Capricorn*

DESCRIPTION Here we are shown a "demonic" man and woman bound by chains to a pedestal, upon which sits a gloating, torch-bearing Devil. The Devil has the head and horns of a goat, the wings of a bat, the ears of a donkey, and the claws of an eagle. The Devil's pedestal is a half cube, indicating that he is lord of half truths and ignorance. In the western esoteric tradition the Devil personifies our own ignorance—we have no adversary other than ourselves. Even the Devil's form, as shown here, has a sense of parody about it. The naked man and woman who are prisoners of the Devil are shown with small horns protruding from their heads—a mark of bestiality. This reminds us that the last vestiges of our animal nature have to be resolved as part of our spiritual journey, for unless we confront these aspects of ourselves we will remain prisoners to worldly materialism and the selfish forces of the ego, or false self.

SPIRITUAL INTERPRETATION In this context, Capricorn the Goat represents darkness and bestiality. The Devil reflects the plight of all unenlightened human beings, with their limited knowledge and understanding. Nevertheless, this Tarot path links to Tiphareth—so all is not lost. Like Death, the Tarot card of the Devil is a path of transition.

IN A TAROT SPREAD This card signifies that your current preoccupations are with worldly, material concerns. It can also mean that you are clinging compulsively to beliefs or values that are limited and are holding you back. You are restricted by your fears and you do not trust your inner spiritual guidance. You may also be subject to various temptations, unethical behavior, and the inappropriate use of force. You have become a victim of your vanity and pride.

REVERSE MEANING You have removed the obstacles that have impeded your path, and can now see a way forward. You have overcome your emotional shortcomings and have found your inner truth. You can see through the shallow nature of material pride and vanity.

SELF-DEVELOPMENT LESSON The Devil personifies our own ignorance and delusion, our false dependence on worldly appearances. The Devil can block our path to spiritual awakening, but only if we allow him to do so.

WORKBOOK EXERCISES

1. Spend a few minutes meditating or reflecting on the following words:

   Darkness surrounds me.
   I explore the darkness within.
   I sense that within this darkness there is light, hope, and freedom.
   I move through the darkness to embrace the light.
2. What are the worst things you can imagine happening to anyone? Write them down. Do you personally know anyone to whom these things have happened?
3. List your five darkest fears. Do you believe these fears come from some sort of external source, or are they within your own being? Rate these fears on a scale of one to ten.
4. Give your fears a human form and personality—maybe imagine them created out of clay or some other malleable substance. Make them specific—add spikes, barbs, jagged teeth, or other scary features. Give them a name. Now do a visualization exercise. Hold each form in your mind's eye and imagine that a fierce wind has arisen. It is blowing each fear away in turn, limb by limb and bit by bit. Imagine at the same time that you are feeling stronger as each fear is diminished. Now imagine yourself enveloped in a healing glow of pure white light. When you open your eyes, you will feel revitalized.

KEY XVI: THE TOWER

Hebrew Path: *Peh* **Ruling Planet**: *Mars*

DESCRIPTION A lightning flash strikes the upper turrets of the Tower, causing it to crumble. The crown at the top of the Tower is dislodged, and two figures—a man and a woman—are shown falling to their deaths on the jagged rocks below. Twenty-two sparks of light—each one the Hebrew letter **Yod**—fill the sky. These represent the twenty-two letters of the Hebrew alphabet and the twenty-two Tarot cards of the Major Arcana. The Tower is built of brick and represents an attempt by humans to scale the heavens. As with the Tower of Babel, however, such efforts prove to be of no avail when based on false pride and worldly ambition. The true Tower of mystical attainment is based on the solid foundations of spiritual truth, and this card serves as a warning that vanity, pride, and human arrogance will prove to be a shaky alternative.

SPIRITUAL INTERPRETATION As a Tarot path upon the Tree of Life, the Tower reaches right up to the highest sphere of Kether—symbolically, it embraces the entire mystical universe (the Crown shown on this card is associated symbolically with Kether). The Tower serves as a reminder that humility is required on the inner journey, and that the influx of divine energy from the higher realms of the Tree will prove too overwhelming unless our inner sense of self is well balanced and has a solid foundation. The Tower is ruled by Mars, who ruthlessly destroys ignorance and vain conceptions.

IN A TAROT SPREAD Drawing this card signifies that your current plans and projects are selfish and will come to nothing. You find yourself in a situation of conflict and change that could have catastrophic consequences. Everything you have taken for granted is about to be challenged.

REVERSE MEANING The process of change has already begun. Go with the flow and do not try to resist what will happen as a consequence. If you are suppressing feelings of grief, anger, or disappointment, let these feelings go and your life will soon change for the better.

SELF-DEVELOPMENT LESSON Essentially, this card is all about overcoming vain and selfish ambition. If we build monuments to ourselves, we will inevitably be disappointed, and any success will be short-lived. However, if we place our lives on a firm spiritual foundation and align our purpose with the will of the cosmos, our destiny will have a positive outcome.

WORKBOOK EXERCISES

1. Spend a few minutes meditating or reflecting on the following words:

   I seek to destroy whatever illusions have been influencing my life and rebuild from a position of strength.
   I seek to place my life upon firm and positive foundations.
   I seek to align my hopes and ambitions with a higher spiritual purpose.
2. In your Tarot journal, make a list of ten things you would like to achieve in the next five years.
3. In your list, how many of these things are intended primarily for your own benefit, and how many have the potential to benefit other people as well?
4. How vulnerable are you to pride and vanity? Make a list of ten things you are really proud of—things that you feel make you stand out above the crowd. Now take another look at your list. How many of these things really matter in the long term? Give yourself a vanity score on a scale of one to ten.
5. Make a new list of five areas of personal interests and activities where your skills could be put to the benefit of the community as a whole.

KEY XVII: THE STAR

Hebrew Path: *Tzaddi* **Ruling Sign**: *Aquarius*

DESCRIPTION A beautiful naked maiden kneels beside a pool of water. Her right foot is placed inside the pool, indicating that she is connected to the watery sphere of the emotions, while her left foot is placed on the earth, demonstrating that she can transmit her intuitive powers to the physical world. She pours the waters of Life from two flasks, one held in each hand. One of these flasks is made of gold (representing the Sun) and the other of silver (the Moon). Above the naked maiden seven silver-white stars glow in the sky, and these represent the seven planets of traditional astrology—Saturn, Mars, Jupiter, Sun, Venus, Moon, and Mercury—while a larger golden star dominates the heavens. This star represents cosmic energy and has eight points, the number Eight signifying the balance of opposing forces. The ground around the pool looks fertile and in the distance we see a mountain, symbolic of the mystic quest. On top of the mountain is a solitary tree, and in this tree sits a scarlet ibis, representing pure thought.

SPIRITUAL INTERPRETATION The Star is associated with intuition, meditation, and the hidden qualities of Nature, represented by the sphere of Netzach on the Tree of Life. Drawing her inspiration from the golden star that dominates the sky, the Star Goddess transmits precious life energy from the golden star down to the world below.

IN A TAROT SPREAD Drawing the Star signifies hope, inspiration, and good health.

Everything about this card is positive—you have been truly blessed. You will receive the gifts of love and spiritual guidance, your life will be filled with purpose and happiness, and your intuitive powers will be greatly enhanced.

REVERSE MEANING You demonstrate a lack of judgement. Ill health lurks on the horizon. You are without a sense of personal direction. Your friends and lovers will abandon you, and you may also incur other forms of loss.

SELF-DEVELOPMENT LESSON When we are a vehicle for the cosmic life energy, our life is filled with abundance and promise. When we trust the guidance of our inner light, our powers of love and creativity flow forth in the world.

WORKBOOK EXERCISES

1. Spend a few minutes meditating or reflecting on the following words:

   I seek to become a vehicle for the cosmic life force.
   The energies of life flow through me and nourish the world around me.
   I welcome guidance from my inner light of Spirit.
2. Make a list of five ways in which you are able to express your creativity.
3. For each of these expressions of creativity, draw up a five-point strategy list for expanding and developing these pursuits so they can reach new horizons in the years ahead.
4. Use this affirmation as part of your daily practice: I am open to new creative solutions for my life. Draw up a five-point list showing how you can share each of your creative gifts with at least one other person.
5. Practice the white light meditation in which you become a vessel for healing light. Relax and feel pure white light moving gradually through every part of your body—from your head down through your neck into your chest, abdomen, legs, and finally reaching the soles of your feet. Feel all of your body glistening with pure white light. Affirm to yourself that you are a vehicle for the sacred light—just like the Star Goddess.

KEY XVIII: THE MOON

Hebrew Path: *Qoph* **Ruling Sign**: *Pisces*

DESCRIPTION Two dogs—one of them domesticated, the other untamed and wolflike—are shown barking at the Moon. The Moon itself is shown both in its full and first-quarter aspects, and shines its light down on two castle turrets, representing humans' domain. In the foreground is a large pool of water representing the waters of Life and, by extension, the powers of the subconscious mind from which creative ideas emerge. Sparks of light float down through the night sky like drops of dew, each of them in the shape of the Hebrew letter Yod.

SPIRITUAL INTERPRETATION The lunar crescent dominates the imagery of the Moon and mirrors the symbolism of the lunar sphere Yesod on the Tree of Life—a sphere associated with dreams, fertility, and the astral imagery of the subconscious mind. The dogs baying at the Moon are sacred to the dark lunar goddess Hecate and we are reminded that traditionally the Moon is associated with dark or hidden forces. The Moon symbolizes the unceasing cycles of change, including the ebb and flow of the biological and psychic tides affecting fertility and creativity, respectively.

IN A TAROT SPREAD This card is associated with intuition, dreams, and the manifestation of psychic powers. If you draw this card, you should be especially alert to subtle changes manifesting in your everyday life—but don't allow yourself to be deceived by appearances. Trust the messages you receive through your dreams and heed the inner voice of your intuition. Recognize too that, like all other sentient beings, you are a force of Nature and you have your wild, untamed side. This means that you may have to acknowledge aspects of your animal nature and at the same time confront your personal demons.

REVERSE MEANING Practicalities are of more importance than intuition or hunches. Don't take any risks at the moment. Wait until storms blow over—a period of upheaval is coming to an end. If someone is trying to deceive you, don't worry. His or her strategies will be exposed.

SELF-DEVELOPMENT LESSON Trust your own spontaneous feelings and your powers of intuition. Heed the messages in your dreams.

WORKBOOK EXERCISES

1. Spend a few minutes meditating or reflecting on the following words:

   I honor my powers of intuition and visionary awakening.
   I honor the cycles of change in Nature and everyday life.
   I welcome the mysteries and secrets of the Night—may they bring me wisdom and understanding.
2. In your Tarot journal, write down a list of three significant ways in which you have had to change course or shift your orientation in the last five years.
3. How open are you to change? Do you prefer to stay with your routines, or do you welcome new ways of doing things? Give yourself a rating of your openness to change, on a scale of one to ten.
4. Practice any of the following positive affirmations that you feel applies to you:
   - I can relax and let go of my fear of change.
   - I am open to new, creative solutions for my life.
   - I can allow myself to go with the flow.
5. Start a dream journal, which is separate from your Tarot journal, and each day record the lessons or messages that emerge from your dreams for a month. If you find this worthwhile, keep recording your dreams as part of an ongoing practice.

KEY XIX: THE SUN

Hebrew Path: *Resh* **Ruling Planet**: *Sun*

DESCRIPTION A radiant Sun shines down upon a naked child riding a horse. The child holds in its hand a large red banner signifying positive action, and also wears a wreath of flowers and a red feather. The child represents the path to liberation and spiritual illumination—symbolically they are one and the same—and we are reminded that even the greatest mystical adept has to become innocent and humble like a child before attaining a state of enlightenment. The horse is a symbol of solar energy, and the young rider does not have a saddle or bridle, indicating a state of perfect balance. Behind the horse and rider is the domain of humans, represented by a brick wall and a cultivated garden. Four large sunflowers are clearly visible, and represent the four elements of Air, Earth, Fire, and Water, as well as the four kingdoms of Nature: mineral, vegetable, animal, and human.

SPIRITUAL INTERPRETATION The Sun reflects the light of Tiphareth, located at the very heart of the Tree of Life. The overall theme of the card is one of positive attainment and the quest for spiritual illumination. There is also a suggestion here that a state of innocence and purity will be attained in the mystical quest for unity with God. This card is clearly ruled by the Sun, representing unity and vitality—the power that sustains Nature.

IN A TAROT SPREAD This is a very positive card to draw in a spread. It signifies joy and happiness as well as success, positive attainment, and good health. Your relationships will be blessed with shared happiness and prosperity; your efforts are coming to fruition. This is also a time to explore your creativity and positive new ideas for the future, for they will flourish when you are in touch with the vitalizing and nurturing force of your inner spiritual Sun.

REVERSE MEANING Right now your future is clouded and unclear. You may suffer a serious loss or fail in your endeavors. Your relationships are in a state of jeopardy—an engagement is likely to be broken or there may be trouble in your marriage. This is a time to pause and take a realistic account of your life and ask yourself where you are headed.

SELF-DEVELOPMENT LESSON When we are guided by the spiritual Sun, we journey toward a state of illumination and humility. We seek a return to a state of innocence and Oneness within the realm of Spirit.

WORKBOOK EXERCISES

1. Spend a few minutes meditating or reflecting on the following words:

   I welcome the guiding light of the Sun.
   I bring light to my journey through life.
   I journey toward greater wisdom and spiritual illumination.

2. In your Tarot journal, list five qualities that you believe contribute to your sense of personal vitality.
3. Where do you think your journey through life is taking you? List three possible options for your life: a) one year from now, b) five years from now, and c) twenty years from now.
4. List five ways in which you feel connected with the powers of Nature. Name your five favorite flowers.
5. List three ways in which your life could serve a spiritual purpose in the years ahead.

KEY XX: JUDGEMENT

Hebrew Path: *Shin* **Ruling Planet**: *Pluto*

DESCRIPTION Groups of naked people rise from their coffins, holding their arms up in the air in celebration at the prospect of new life. Above them is the archangel Gabriel with his trumpet. He wears a blue robe and represents the element of Water. Here he also personifies the Divine Breath that calls forth the living in the Last Judgement. His banner bears the symbol of the cross of spiritual redemption. Away on the horizon, snow-capped mountains symbolize the mystic quest. The child in the foreground has turned his back to us and is facing the mountains in the distance, indicating that in a state of mystical innocence he is embracing the source of spiritual wisdom and understanding. This Tarot path is ruled by Pluto, Lord of the Underworld and the abode of the dead. This card represents spiritual awakening and renewal.

SPIRITUAL INTERPRETATION However, the Tarot card of Judgement reminds us that in the mystical teachings death leads to spiritual rebirth. Here the human figures rising from their coffins are gesturing with their arms to embrace the power of the Holy Spirit as they rise in triumph from the "grave" of ignorance. Gabriel is sounding his trumpet to herald their spiritual awakening. This card represents the triumph of rebirth—return to the Spirit.

IN A TAROT SPREAD On a metaphysical level this card represents spiritual awakening and renewal. In the context of your everyday affairs, however, it signifies that good things are about to happen in your life. You are called to experience something new and exciting, and this may mean leaving your old thoughts and conditioning behind. You will enjoy better health, you will feel reinvigorated and more alert, and you can now go forward with renewed clarity and vision. Your perspective on life is much broader than it was before.

REVERSE MEANING You are sinking in a pool of negative emotions—you feel a strong sense of shame and remorse. You fear death. You have turned your back on the spiritual side of life. You may experience ill health or serious personal loss. On the positive side, if you heed the guidance from your inner spiritual voice, you may be able to release the negativity in which you have immersed yourself, and redeem the situation.

SELF-DEVELOPMENT LESSON We die to our old selves and are reborn anew. We emerge from the darkness of our ignorance as we embrace the light of new understanding and wisdom. We are truly reborn when we enter the realm of Spirit.

WORKBOOK EXERCISES

1. Spend a few minutes meditating or reflecting on the following words:

   I leave behind my old, limited, and constricted self.
   I open my heart and mind to new life and vitality.
   I embrace the healing, uplifting power of the Spirit.
2. In your Tarot journal, make a list of five things about yourself that you would like to discard and replace with more positive human qualities.
3. List three ways in which your attitudes and beliefs have held you back from acting positively during the past year. Consider the list once again. What strategies can you come up with to help you move beyond the limitations of these negative attitudes?
4. Write down three occasions when you experienced considerable personal loss. What were your feelings on those occasions? Now write down three ways in which your experiences of personal loss can also lead to a broader spiritual perspective and a greater understanding of life as a whole.

KEY XXI: THE WORLD

Hebrew Path: *Tau* **Ruling Planet**: *Saturn*

DESCRIPTION A beautiful maiden, clad only in a long flowing scarf, dances within a wreath of leaves. She holds a wand in each hand. The dancing maiden is known in the Kabbalah as the Bride, although her sphere is also referred to as the Kingdom. The World therefore incorporates both male and female polarities.

Significantly, although the dancing figure reveals her breasts, her genitals are covered by the scarf, disguising the fact that she is androgynous. She is the counterpart of the Fool at the very top of the Tree of Life, a figure who is similarly androgynous—the fusion of male and female principles symbolizing the unity of opposites or the attainment of mystical unity. This dancer represents both the attainment of cosmic consciousness and the first steps upon the mystic quest.

SPIRITUAL INTERPRETATION The World is both a beginning and an ending, for the creative dance expressing the relationship between essence and form is infinite. To regain an awareness of mystical unity, the spiritual journey begins in the everyday world and leads back through the different spheres of the Tree of Life to their source in the Oneness of *Ain Soph Aur*, the Limitless Light.

IN A TAROT SPREAD This card represents personal rewards and the fulfillment of all desires. It is a card of triumph, happiness, and success. Drawing this card in a spread signifies that you can move ahead with confidence. It also represents personal freedom and the exploration of new horizons. In terms of your personal relationships, while you are feeling happy and secure in your present situation, this may also be the beginning of a new phase in your partnership.

REVERSE MEANING You have not yet learned life's lessons. You lack a vision for your life, and are yet to taste the fruits of success. You are reluctant to explore new opportunities, and your fears may lead you into a state of lethargy or stagnation.

SELF-DEVELOPMENT LESSON Our world is as large and as bountiful as we can imagine it to be. Our horizons need no boundaries. We are in this world to experience the lessons of life.

WORKBOOK EXERCISES

1. Spend a few minutes meditating or reflecting on the following words:
   I embrace the World and give thanks for my life here on Earth.
   I honor the Sacred Maiden whose dance is the Dance of Life.
   I seek my life's true spiritual purpose.
2. In your Tarot journal, list five ways in which you are benefiting from your everyday life. Now list five ways in which you can share those benefits with others.
3. Does your life have a spiritual purpose? In ten lines or less, write down in your journal a concise summary of your spiritual purpose as you see it today. You might like to return to this in a year, or even five years from now, to see how your understanding of your spiritual purpose matures and develops with the passage of time.
4. Review all twenty-two Tarot cards of the Major Arcana in this chapter. Consider them in the sequence as they are presented here—as symbols of the sacred and infinite Spirit gradually becoming manifest and present in the World.
5. Now consider the twenty-two Tarot cards of the Major Arcana in reverse sequence—from the World back to the Fool. Reflect on the idea that these cards represent your mystical pathway back to the source of Creation, back to the sacred origins of life itself.

CHAPTER FIVE

THE CARDS OF THE MINOR ARCANA

This section provides a description for all cards in the four Tarot suits and their meanings.

ACE OF WANDS

DESCRIPTION One rod, or club, roughly hewn is held vertically aloft by a hand that emerges from clouds. The castle on a distant hill represents the promise of things to come. *Element: Fire*

INTERPRETATION A card of creativity and fresh beginnings, it suggests a new journey—a new career, a new business, or a major change in lifestyle. This card may herald an inheritance, a new direction in your personal relationships, or the birth of a child.

REVERSE MEANING Be cautious—watch carefully and take stock of the situation you are in. An act of selfishness could spoil a new business venture, or other unforeseen circumstances could provide a setback. You may not have enough drive to see a project through to completion.

SELF-DEVELOPMENT LESSON This is a card of imagination, creative energy, and initiative, and reminds us that we all have great potential.

WORKBOOK EXERCISES

1. List three important decisions for change you have made in your life.
2. How have these undertakings influenced the way your life has unfolded?

TWO OF WANDS

DESCRIPTION A cloaked figure faces away from us. Flanked by two vertical wands, representing enterprise and prosperity, this is either a merchant or an owner of property, and he is watching the horizon in the expectation that his ships will come into port fully laden. On the battlements of his castle, the white lilies represent pure thought, the red roses desire. The figure here has a well-balanced temperament, for he embodies clarity of purpose and passionate intent. *Element: Fire.*

INTERPRETATION This card represents achievement in business. A contract or new business partnership is about to eventuate. Your plans will bear fruit. You have considerable ability and also foresight—but you will also need to demonstrate perseverance in order to succeed. This card may also represent human kindness and an interest in the sciences.

REVERSE MEANING All the good work you have put into your planned project may come to nothing. Be cautious, and guard against impatience. Take care to prevent others from dominating you.

SELF-DEVELOPMENT LESSON We can build strong and fruitful relationships with other people, but we also have to establish our own identities. Courage and foresight can bring positive rewards.

WORKBOOK EXERCISES

1. Think of three ways in which business decisions you have made have borne fruit.
2. How big a part did your perseverance play in the outcomes?

THREE OF WANDS

DESCRIPTION The merchant from the Two of Wands surveys the horizon. We can see his ships coming closer. He holds one of the three wands firmly with his right hand. He has staked his claim and now awaits a positive outcome, one that reflects all the hard work that has been undertaken. *Element: Fire*

INTERPRETATION This card represents partnership and cooperation in business transactions. Someone will come forward and offer assistance to you, or you will find a partner for an important business undertaking. Finding the right partner will bring you prosperity.

REVERSE MEANING Carelessness, or misplaced confidence without attention to detail, could spoil everything. Your personal energy is scattered rather than focused. Watch out for excessive pride or arrogance, because such an attitude could cause your undoing.

SELF-DEVELOPMENT LESSON Do not congratulate yourself on achieving success before seeing your venture through every stage on its path to completion. A solid basis is required for anything to prosper. Make good use of your skills and build your house on firm foundations.

WORKBOOK EXERCISES

1. List five occasions in your life when partnership has led to success.
2. Why was the factor of partnership so significant?

FOUR OF WANDS

DESCRIPTION The four wands in the foreground are decorated with garlands of flowers that make a type of canopy. Two figures approach, holding bouquets of flowers in celebration. Behind them is a large bridge adjoining a turreted castle. *Element: Fire*

INTERPRETATION This is a card representing balance, peace, and prosperity—and a job well done. It can also signify recovery from hardship, or a period of consolidation following a period of protracted effort. You may need to regain your strength before proceeding to the next stage. Nevertheless, you should feel free to enjoy the results of the hard work you have undertaken. This card signifies that your relationships are stable and that romance may lead to marriage.

REVERSE MEANING With a positive attitude you will achieve a good outcome. Learn to appreciate the benefits of everyday life and find comfort in the support of friends and family.

SELF-DEVELOPMENT LESSON In between the struggles involved in making your relationships work, take time to celebrate your positive achievements. Apply yourself to learning everything you can from peace and stability. Be gentle rather than aggressive—for there is strength in gentleness as well.

WORKBOOK EXERCISES

1. Think of three occasions when you have come through a period of extended effort to achieve a solid result.
2. What was the most satisfying aspect of each of these personal achievements?

FIVE OF WANDS

DESCRIPTION Five young men are engaging with each other in conflict and using the five rods, or wands, as weapons. This card symbolizes a test or struggle of some kind; however, as wands themselves are associated with enterprise and success, the conflict is not necessarily negative—it may be some kind of challenge. *Element: Fire*

INTERPRETATION The number Five is associated with uncertainty. On this card, competitive—and possibly combative—forces have been unleashed. The Five of Wands is sometimes known as the Lord of Strife. Perhaps you are engaged in a quarrel or dispute with a neighbor, or have entered into a process of aggressive litigation. Alternatively, you are facing a barrage of obstacles. Nevertheless, a willingness to be firm and stand up for yourself could certainly produce a positive outcome.

REVERSE MEANING Peace and harmony, rather than conflict, are indicated. Your relationships are stable and harmonious, and life presents new opportunities that you can take up as a challenge.

SELF-DEVELOPMENT LESSON Even if you are feeling the pressure of mounting stress, draw on your inner reserves of strength and retain your clarity. Face the challenge of competition, reassess your existing attitudes, and always watch out for new opportunities within the struggles of everyday life.

WORKBOOK EXERCISES

1. Think of three events in your life that you associated with considerable uncertainty.
2. What reserves of strength did you draw on to help you pull through?

SIX OF WANDS

DESCRIPTION We see a man of authority riding on horseback. He holds a staff, or wand, bearing a wreath of laurel, and he wears a similar wreath on his head. He is victorious, for he rides beside his foot soldiers in an act of triumph. *Element: Fire*

INTERPRETATION Victory is assured. Your efforts will bring success. Keep persisting in whatever field of activity you are engaged in, because you will win in the end. You may also have strong leadership potential. The number Six also expresses reconciliation, so clearly your relationships will improve and reflect this potential for equilibrium.

REVERSE MEANING Bad news is coming. A competitor may prove victorious at your expense. Your success is being postponed or thwarted, and things you have been striving for are beginning to fall apart.

SELF-DEVELOPMENT LESSON Persistent effort will be rewarded, but take care not to remain too long on your high horse or to look down on others. Learn to accept the contribution of others who are willing to support your work and ideas. Value your friends.

WORKBOOK EXERCISES

1. List three occasions when your success came at someone else's expense.
2. How would you act differently now?

SEVEN OF WANDS

DESCRIPTION A young man is fighting with a staff, and six opponents are proving a major obstacle. Although these adversaries are not depicted on the card—only their staffs are shown in the foreground—the young man clearly has a fight on his hands. *Element: Fire*

INTERPRETATION You must draw on your inner resources as well as your physical strength in order to fight against adversity. Your success will depend on personal resolve and courage. If you are involved in a business transaction, be aware that you face some stiff competition. In your personal relationships, you will need to clarify some specific issues that present an ongoing problem. Even if you currently have the advantage in your personal relationships, you may need to negotiate a mutual settlement.

REVERSE MEANING Don't allow other people to take advantage of you. Remain patient and avoid indecision.

SELF-DEVELOPMENT LESSON It is often said, "He who hesitates is lost." Don't let others take advantage of you, and trust your inner reserves—your creative energy and your intuition. There are times when we all have to hold firm to what we believe in.

WORKBOOK EXERCISES

1. How confident are you in situations where you feel stiff competition surrounding you on all sides? List three such situations where this has been the case, and how the situation made you feel.
2. Recall the way you dealt with your anxieties on these occasions. Would you act differently now?

EIGHT OF WANDS

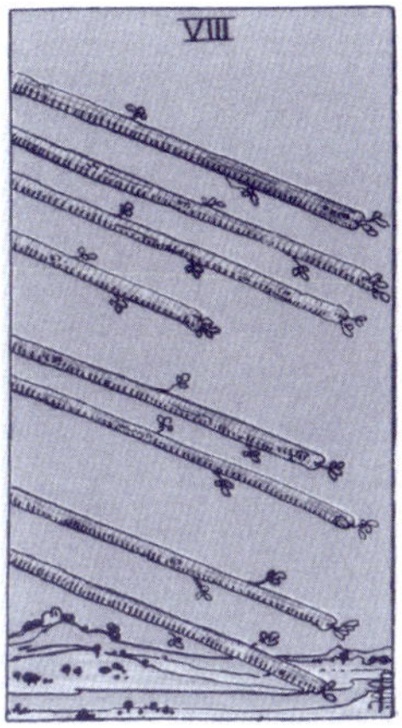

DESCRIPTION Eight wands are shown in parallel formation, stretching at an angle across the sky. We can see the land below, but no human figures are depicted on this card. The eight wands are rather like "message sticks" of communication and are shown reaching across the visible universe, inviting us to heed their call. *Element: Fire*

INTERPRETATION The number Eight represents the balance of opposing forces, but we are also reminded to reconsider previous decisions and to take stock of the existing situation. Here we are approaching a goal. Because the sky is a specific feature of this card, a journey through the air—a business trip interstate or overseas—is a distinct possibility. But it may also be the case that things are up in the air at the moment, and you must be decisive in order to produce a satisfactory outcome.

REVERSE MEANING Insecurity, jealousy, violence, quarrels, and domestic arguments are indicated. The message you are waiting for will fail to arrive.

SELF-DEVELOPMENT LESSON Wait patiently to see how things play out, rather than rushing ahead carelessly. When you are presented with various options, weigh the consequences carefully so the choices you make will be appropriate to the given situation.

WORKBOOK EXERCISES

1. Think of three occasions when you had to act as a mediator between people holding contrary points of view. How did you help resolve these problems?
2. What qualities do you associate with acts of mediation?

NINE OF WANDS

DESCRIPTION A man stands facing us. He is holding a staff somewhat defensively, as if guarding his territory. Eight other staffs behind him provide a barrier or blockade. The man has a bandage on his head, indicating that he has been involved in previous conflicts and must now stand ready once again to fight for what he believes in. *Element: Fire*

INTERPRETATION You are ready to protect your existing situation and you may well achieve success—but not without further struggle. Stay true to what you believe and draw on your powers of discretion, but avoid becoming obstinate as you hold your ground. In terms of your personal relationships, this card indicates that you may be carrying the wounds of the past—previous abuse in a parent–child relationship or some form of emotional attack—but you have gained a certain wisdom from experience and this will see you through.

REVERSE MEANING You lack initiative. You are unprepared and vulnerable. You refuse to stand up for what is right, and bend in the face of attack.

SELF-DEVELOPMENT LESSON Draw strength from your wounds—from past emotional struggles and attacks. You will become ever more resourceful if you learn to weather adversity. Trust your own reserves of strength and character, for these will help you to see things through.

WORKBOOK EXERCISES

1. List three situations in which you have allowed your obstinacy to get the better of you.
2. How did your obstinacy complicate the situation in each case? Can you think of better ways to resolve these problems?

TEN OF WANDS

DESCRIPTION A young man clutches a heavy bunch of ten flowering staffs. Although he is fully extended physically, he walks steadfastly toward his home in the distance. The number Ten symbolizes perfection through completion. *Element: Fire*

INTERPRETATION Your determination and resolve will pay off because you have laid the foundation for the next step along your life's journey. However, you feel that your present load is heavy—either physically or emotionally. You are very much under pressure and you have experienced many changes, all of which are now coming to a head. The number Ten represents endings and beginnings, so this could be the closing phase of your past cycle, with fresh new opportunities still to come. You may also need to ask yourself, though, whether you actually enjoy the weight of heavy responsibility or fixed beliefs. This may be an ideal time to trust the help and advice of others whose opinions you value.

REVERSE MEANING Your talents and skills are being used the wrong way. You have applied your strength and creative energy to selfish goals, and you also show a tendency to shift the burdens of responsibility unfairly onto other people.

SELF-DEVELOPMENT LESSON Irrespective of the burdens you carry alone in life, there are also times when it is useful to heed the advice and help of others whom you trust. When your personal burdens seem oppressive, take the time to reevaluate your life in order to ensure that you are still on the right course.

WORKBOOK EXERCISE

1. Think of an occasion when you felt under pressure and were helped out by a friend. Could you act this way yourself? List three characteristics of personal inner strength.

PAGE OF WANDS

DESCRIPTION The Page can be a child of either gender, and this card has been referred to as both the Princess of the Shining Flame and the Rose of the Palace of Fire. The Page of Wands is a shining figure, attired in a richly embellished jacket and cloak and holding a wand aloft. Here the wand is an emblem of royal authority, and we sense that the Page is about to deliver an important message. *Element: Earth of Fire*

INTERPRETATION The Page of Wands represents the person who finds himself or herself at the center of events and has a burning desire to achieve great things. Causes are pursued vigorously. This card is associated with brilliance, enthusiasm, and courage. The Page is a bearer of tidings, so it is very likely that a relative or friend has some important or happy news for you. Expect a letter, e-mail, or telephone call soon. It is apparent that you are open to new ideas and suggestions from others.

REVERSE MEANING When the Page of Wands is reversed, expect bad news. You may also find yourself unable to commit to the tasks ahead, and you may allow your personal relationships to suffer through neglect.

SELF-DEVELOPMENT LESSON Heed the messenger. Focus on new initiatives and remain open to input from others. Remember to bear your load of responsibility in your personal relationships.

WORKBOOK EXERCISES

1. List three happy occasions when you received good news.
2. What did you feel on these occasions and why were they so significant for you?

KNIGHT OF WANDS

DESCRIPTION We are shown a young knight riding his horse. He looks impressive in his shining armor and plumed helmet. The garment he is wearing is decorated with salamanders—the elemental spirits associated with Fire—and his title is Lord of Flame and Lightning. He holds a staff, or wand, in his right hand. Three mountain peaks are visible in the distance. *Element: Fire of Fire*

INTERPRETATION This figure embodies energy and dynamism—the power, drive, and determination to achieve what one wants. But the Knight of Wands has an impetuous nature and often plunges in too quickly when pursuing his goals. In terms of romantic involvements, this card can signal the beginning of a sexual affair that lacks commitment. More generally, however, this card indicates that sudden changes may be just around the corner; this could be the start or end of something significant.

REVERSE MEANING Your work is being disrupted. You are frustrated and restricted by minor obstacles. Narrow-mindedness and suspicion rule the day. Your friend or lover is jealous of you.

SELF-DEVELOPMENT LESSON It requires power and commitment to achieve our aims in life—but do we also have the necessary patience to see our goals through to fruition? We should avoid hasty, impetuous decisions; we also need to follow our consciences as we plan our actions.

WORKBOOK EXERCISES

1. What are your own sources of dynamic energy? Are they physical, mental, or emotional?
2. Make a list of your present dynamic qualities and also those you would like to achieve.

QUEEN OF WANDS

DESCRIPTION The dignified monarch sits on her throne. Indeed, her title is Queen of the Thrones of Flame. She is mature and self-possessed but also an accessible and popular ruler. She holds a staff in her right hand and a sunflower in her left, the latter symbolizing her affinity with the world of Nature. Lions are engraved on the arms of her throne, reminding us of her connection with the astrological sign of Leo. A black cat, a symbol of power and restraint, is also visible in the foreground. *Element: Water of Fire*

INTERPRETATION The Queen of Wands is an authoritative leader, and her judgements are honorable and well considered. She is sensible, generous, and helpful to her followers. If you draw this card you have a stable disposition and can act with both courage and authority. Your personal relationships are based on a mature understanding, and you are both loyal and insightful. Although you are strict, you are also fair.

REVERSE MEANING You are inclined to be narrow-minded, obstinate, and domineering. There is also a clear chance of jealousy and deceit.

SELF-DEVELOPMENT LESSON Explore the sources of your personal power and set your own limits. If you are a woman, you will feel secure in your emotional needs; if you are a man, you are already in touch with the feminine aspects of your personality and recognize them as a source of inspiration.

WORKBOOK EXERCISES

1. When you think of people who command respect and authority, what is it that sets them apart?
2. List five contemporary leaders who command your respect. Why do you admire them?

KING OF WANDS

DESCRIPTION The King of Wands sits on his impressive throne, surveying his kingdom. Symbols of Fire—salamanders and lions—decorate the pillar behind him, and a small salamander also sits at his feet. He has a staff in his right hand. *Element: Air of Fire*

INTERPRETATION The King is a mature and respected leader, and he is both passionate and generous by nature. This card is associated with sound business acumen and wise judgement, as well as financial prosperity. In drawing this card, you clearly display strong leadership qualities. The success you have achieved in life has been well earned.

REVERSE MEANING You are inclined to be strict and intolerant, and somewhat authoritarian in your relationships with others. You are easily drawn into arguments, you allow your prejudices to show, and you may feel uneasy in your business transactions.

SELF-DEVELOPMENT LESSON It is important that you learn to explore and understand views that are different from your own. Seek to overcome any capacity for prejudice and cynicism, and learn from your mistakes. Stay open to the forces of spiritual inspiration that provide you with a natural sense of dynamism and passion.

WORKBOOK EXERCISES

1. What makes a good leader? List five attributes of leadership that you think are important.
2. Which of these qualities do you possess?

ACE OF CUPS

DESCRIPTION A stemmed cup or chalice is held aloft by a hand that emerges from clouds. A dove bearing a wafer in its beak is shown descending over the cup, and five distinct streams of water flow from the brim of the vessel and fall into a lily pond below. Leaves are also falling through the air. *Element: Water*

INTERPRETATION The number One represents beginnings, and this chalice is a symbol of the fountain of life. The dove represents Spirit, and the streams of water that flow from the cup symbolize the five senses. The world is being nourished by the Spirit. This point in time is the beginning of all things good—especially love, joy, beauty, and health. It may also signify a new development in your spiritual understanding.

REVERSE MEANING At present you are closed to experiences of the heart and too caught up in the selfish concerns of the ego. You are too self-centered to appreciate the concerns of others.

SELF-DEVELOPMENT LESSON You must move beyond your self-centered concerns to realize your true spiritual potential. Spirit nourishes all things. Open yourself to this higher wisdom and welcome it into your heart.

WORKBOOK EXERCISES

1. List three ways in which you can do more to overcome your self-centeredness and open yourself more to spiritual concerns.
2. Which of these is the most important in your life right now?

TWO OF CUPS

DESCRIPTION A man and woman pledge their troth of love and dedication to each other. They each hold a chalice. Above them is the winged head of a lion and immediately below, surmounting the two chalices, is a caduceus with intertwining serpents. *Element: Water*

INTERPRETATION This card represents the bond of love between two people. This can be interpreted as a formal marriage, an agreement of mutual cooperation, or simply a state of harmony in which two people happily dwell. It is a card representing equilibrium and understanding, and reminds us that through mutual support we can attain our goals. The caduceus was traditionally the staff carried by Hermes, or Mercury—messenger of the gods—and represents the balance between Heaven and Earth. The winged lion epitomizes the fusion of Spirit and brute strength. This card represents the beginning of new love or friendship and also the sharing of positive ideas for the future.

REVERSE MEANING Your relationships have fallen out of balance. Disagreement is raising obstacles to progress. Love has turned to hate and despair.

SELF-DEVELOPMENT LESSON Honor and respect the contributions of both individuals in your loving partnership. Kindness and mutual consideration can join your hearts together.

WORKBOOK EXERCISES

1. Take time out to reflect on the bonds of love and friendship you have with other people.
2. How have these bonds helped you in your own life? Have they helped you develop spiritually in new ways?

THREE OF CUPS

DESCRIPTION Three happy young women rejoice and hold cups aloft in celebration. Garlands of flowers lie scattered around their feet. The maidens are making a celebratory toast—to love, abundance, and success. *Element: Water*

INTERPRETATION The number Three represents growth and expression. This card is about rejoicing in our happiness, success, and love—and the sheer joy of being together. It tells of sweet fulfillment and new opportunities still to come. It may also represent the blossoming of new spiritual potential and creative expression in music and the arts. And, because Three flows on from Two, lovers may soon be celebrating the birth of a child.

REVERSE MEANING What once brought joy now brings pain. Your potential for creative growth and spiritual expression remains hidden. You are overindulging yourself and creating problems for yourself rather than building for the future.

SELF-DEVELOPMENT LESSON Create a way to share your happiness, love, and abundance. Celebrations can come from past achievement, but may also signify a happy and fulfilling path ahead. Take stock of your life in a happy, playful way and look ahead for new and welcoming opportunities.

WORKBOOK EXERCISES

1. List five ways in which you express yourself creatively.
2. Think of three further creative activities that you would like to pursue in the future.

FOUR OF CUPS

DESCRIPTION A young man sits cross-legged beneath a tree, his thoughts attuned to deep reflection. In the foreground, three cups are positioned next to each other on the grass. A fourth cup is held in the air by a hand that emerges from a cloud. *Element: Water*

INTERPRETATION This card signifies personal discontent and withdrawal from the everyday world. There is a clear sense of turning away from material success, and here the young man's emotions are turned inward as well. This card is about reviewing and reformulating personal goals and values, and there are signs of hesitancy and self-doubt as well. The inspirational cup that floats in the sky is clearly an offering from the realm of Spirit, but it is by no means certain that the young man will respond to this gift. There is a sense of despondency and a distinct lack of motivation.

REVERSE MEANING Here the reverse meaning is much more positive! New relationships are possible, there is motivation for work and action in the everyday world, and new ambitions are taking shape.

SELF-DEVELOPMENT LESSON We need to take time, both with others and on our own, to reflect on choices in our everyday lives. This requires patience and effort. If we fail to do this, our lives will remain static and lethargic and we will lose any sense of purpose.

WORKBOOK EXERCISES

1. Have you ever sabotaged your own success? List three occasions when you got in your own way.
2. How would you act now, with the benefit of hindsight?

FIVE OF CUPS

DESCRIPTION Although two of the cups remain upright, three others have spilled their contents, and the "wine of life" is splattered onto the earth. A man dressed in a black cloak looks down at the ground in sorrow. The meandering river in the distance finally passes beneath a bridge leading to a forlorn castle. *Element: Water*

INTERPRETATION The number Five represents change and uncertainty, and this card signifies deep sorrow or the loss of a loved one. Perhaps a marriage or other relationship is breaking up. It certainly feels as if life is burdened with disillusionment, and nothing seems worthwhile or pleasurable anymore. Significantly, the figure on this card is paying far more attention to the cups that have spilled than to the two remaining upright. So, although there is loss, potentially there is also hope—but we will have to move beyond our grief and regret in order to embrace new opportunities.

REVERSE MEANING Things are now looking much more hopeful. Old friends or lovers have returned. We muster sufficient courage to move forward.

SELF-DEVELOPMENT LESSON We can sometimes be so overcome with a sense of loss that we forget that all aspects of life are transient. We should always endeavor to move beyond regret and self-recrimination, and have the courage to salvage something worthwhile from our shattered dreams.

WORKBOOK EXERCISE

1. How do you respond to change and uncertainty? List three occasions in your life when you have responded to uncertainty in a negative way, and three occasions when you responded positively. Would you act differently today?

SIX OF CUPS

DESCRIPTION A boy is offering a cup filled with flowers to a little girl. A picturesque village setting, with a thatched cottage and stone tower, is in the background. In the foreground, four cups—also filled with flowers—stand in a row. Another flower-filled cup rests on a nearby podium embellished with a heraldic cross. *Element: Water*

INTERPRETATION This card signifies happiness or pleasant memories based on past acquaintance. Childlike joy stirs in your heart. You may meet an old friend, receive a gift or some unexpected news, or come into an inheritance. The Six of Cups also represents new opportunities—so perhaps you will be offered a job in a new location. In terms of personal relationships, this is also an opportune time to acknowledge the support and encouragement you have received from your partner.

REVERSE MEANING You are living in the past instead of the present. Your ideas and values are outmoded. Rewards you feel you have earned may be delayed. Someone else may receive recognition that you feel should come to you.

SELF-DEVELOPMENT LESSON Reflect on the way you have been enriched by your relationships and by the lessons you have learned from life. But then be prepared to move on—we all have to emerge from the past, live in the present, and be open to what lies ahead.

WORKBOOK EXERCISES

1. To what extent are you able to move on from the past and live in the present? Think of three ways in which you have had to shed past attachments in order to move ahead.
2. Do you still have any lingering tendencies that mean you live in the past and avoid facing the challenges of the present and future? List some of these tendencies—you may need to address them sooner than you think!

SEVEN OF CUPS

DESCRIPTION We see a young man in a visionary state—seven cups rise up before him as if in a dream. He has to choose between them. They contain the head of a beautiful woman, a castle, a cluster of jewels, a writhing snake representing jealousy, a red dragon signifying temptation, and a wreath of victory. In the center of the vision is perhaps the most significant cup of all, for it contains a figure shrouded in a drape. This may be a vision of the young man's future self—his true, as yet unrecognized, spiritual potential. *Element: Water*

INTERPRETATION You are finding it hard to make a clear decision. For the moment you are lost in a fantasy world where your attention flows from one reverie to another. You are being distracted by your dreams instead of taking positive action. Clearly you would be wise to focus on what you really need to achieve. Narrow your options, wake up from your dreams, and do what you have to do. After all, you do have the ability to make a clear choice.

REVERSE MEANING You already have the ability to focus on a specific task or project. You are now on the right track. Pursue your goals.

SELF-DEVELOPMENT LESSON We all have to make choices in life. Learn to make decisions, get your head out of the clouds, and pursue your goals constructively—if you don't, you may be lost in a world of illusion and make-believe.

WORKBOOK EXERCISES

1. How decisive are you when it comes to crunch time? List three occasions in your life when you acted decisively and reached a positive outcome.
2. Now list three occasions when you failed to act decisively and the outcome was unfavorable. What would you do differently today?

EIGHT OF CUPS

DESCRIPTION Eight stacked cups dominate the foreground. A man is walking away from them, turning his back on what they represent, and heading instead for the barren mountains in the distance. He is a solitary traveler and carries nothing but his staff. The Moon is visible in the sky above him and is shown simultaneously full and waning. *Element: Water*

INTERPRETATION You are in the process of rejecting everything you have previously held dear to you. Perhaps you also feel disappointed by your friends and lovers—this may be the right time to move away from a destructive relationship. This is very much a card of transition. It indicates that you are looking for something that's missing in your life. Perhaps you are searching for sources of deeper, inspirational meaning and embarking on a solitary journey toward spiritual fulfillment.

REVERSE MEANING You wish to pursue a more worldly life, and for the moment you have turned your back on spiritual concerns. You are more interested in personal success, good food, and good company. A new lover will soon appear in your life.

SELF-DEVELOPMENT LESSON Open yourself to new possibilities. Allow yourself to be guided by a higher spiritual source.

WORKBOOK EXERCISES

1. Think of three occasions in your life when you faced major disappointment. Write down how you reacted to this disappointment in each case. Would you respond the same way today?
2. If you feel that some of your responses to disappointment were inappropriate, how would you respond to these situations now?

NINE OF CUPS

DESCRIPTION The number Nine signifies summation. Here we are shown a prosperous-looking man sitting smugly in front of nine cups, which are neatly arranged on a shelf behind him. He is content with what he has achieved and accumulated in terms of material possessions—a positive future looks assured. *Element: Water*

INTERPRETATION Sometimes referred to as the "Wish Card," the Nine of Cups represents material success, abundance, and emotional and intellectual contentment. It also signifies physical health and a fondness for sensual pleasures. Your wishes will come true. Drawing this card may also mean that you have several specific plans for the future and you can proceed with confidence. However, the crossed arms of the seated figure remind us to avoid basking in the sweet glow of our success and becoming complacent, and to explore future opportunities.

REVERSE MEANING Overindulgence in food or drink is indicated here. Your wishes will not be fulfilled at this time. You may suffer a setback or deprivation of some sort, such as a lack of money or a change of fortune, although this is unlikely to endure for long.

SELF-DEVELOPMENT LESSON Although this card relates most specifically to material happiness, it is important to remember that true happiness means our emotional and spiritual needs are also being met. Stay in touch with your intuitive side, keep calm and relaxed, and remain open to the positive and creative potentials that are now unfolding in front of you.

WORKBOOK EXERCISE

1. Wishes can come true! Think of three occasions in your life when you wished hard for something to happen and it did. Now make a wish list for the coming year. What are your priorities for the immediate future?

TEN OF CUPS

DESCRIPTION A young married couple stand arm in arm and hold their hands to the heavens in joy. Above them, ten glistening cups arc across the sky like a rainbow of light. Nearby their two children dance happily together, and we can also see the family home in the distance. It looks idyllic, nestling among trees on top of a hill. *Element: Water*

INTERPRETATION The number Ten symbolizes perfection. This card signifies a happy family life and enduring happiness, although here the satisfaction comes not only from material success and emotional security but also from spiritual attunement—for the cups are in formation in the heavens. This card represents a high point in your personal relationships and shows that you are experiencing harmony and integration in all aspects of your life. Your personal hopes and dreams have come true.

REVERSE MEANING This could mean betrayal, family quarrels, sadness, and children turning against parents.

SELF-DEVELOPMENT LESSON The number Ten signifies perfection and completion, but can also mean the beginning of a new cycle. Acknowledge the efforts that you and those around you have made to create the joy and self-fulfillment you are now experiencing, but stay open to new possibilities so your happiness will be ongoing.

WORKBOOK EXERCISES

1. What makes you feel really happy and content? Make a list of ten things.
2. Now put them in order of priority. Take some time to reflect on this list. Are you content with your priorities? Are they consistent with the values you hold?

PAGE OF CUPS

DESCRIPTION This card is known as the Lotus of the Palace of Floods and also as the Princess of the Waters. The Page is holding a single cup containing a fish that has been caught. The Page stands on the ocean shore, looking happy and relaxed. Gently rolling waves can be seen in the distance. *Element: Earth of Water*

INTERPRETATION The element of Water is associated with thoughts, dreams, and emotions. Here a new idea, symbolized by the fish, is being born or taking form, and this is the birth of something special. Traditionally this card is associated with good news, the birth of a child, or the commencement of an exciting new project.

REVERSE MEANING You lack imagination and have become selfish. At present your creative abilities have deserted you.

SELF-DEVELOPMENT LESSON You have overcome obstacles and can see things in a new light. Stay open to receiving help from others—especially from someone young. This is a good time to focus on a particular emotional issue, and this focus will assist your personal growth.

WORKBOOK EXERCISES

1. Write down three occasions in your life when you acted on an exciting new idea. Were you pleased with the outcome? Why?
2. Have there been times when you have let a good idea slip away? How would you act differently today?

KNIGHT OF CUPS

DESCRIPTION This card is known as the Lord of the Waves and the Waters and also as the King of Hosts of the Sea. We are shown a handsome armored knight riding on a horse and bearing a chalice. He appears to be embarking on a quest. In some Tarot decks the crab and peacock attend the Knight—they represent the active, brilliant qualities of the element of Water. *Element: Fire of Water*

INTERPRETATION Drawing this card indicates that you are about to set out on a new mission or receive a new proposal. You may be about to fall in love. You are sufficiently secure emotionally to enter into a new relationship, but take care to ensure that it is genuine. The knight's winged helmet indicates a heightened imaginative awareness, so your new partner may be skilled in the creative arts.

REVERSE MEANING If you have recently received an offer of some kind, check out all the accompanying conditions because it may not be genuine. You are inclined to let your imagination run away with you. Beware of half truths.

SELF-DEVELOPMENT LESSON Look before you leap! Don't get caught up in superficialities. Don't concentrate so much on the outward appearance of a proposal that you fail to heed its content.

WORKBOOK EXERCISES

1. Think of three occasions in your life when you have entered a new relationship (love, business, family, etc.). Write down the feelings you had at the time.
2. Were these feelings—positive or negative—borne out of what later came to pass? Would you respond or act differently today?

QUEEN OF CUPS

DESCRIPTION A beautiful woman—Queen of the Thrones of the Waters—sits pondering the contents of a closed cup that has handles in the form of angels. Its lid hides its contents, indicating that many of the Queen's imaginative impulses are unconscious. Her throne is decorated with water nymphs and rests on a pebbly shore beside the sea. *Element: Water of Water*

INTERPRETATION The Queen is lost in reverie and relies more on her imagination than on common sense. Drawing this card indicates that emotions play an important role in your life at this time, and you may be experiencing a degree of heightened intensity in your personal relationships. You are a loving, gentle person. Your experience is helpful to others and your opinions are valued. However, you are often caught in your own thoughts.

REVERSE MEANING You are perverse and bitter, and inclined to exaggerate. You may not be very reliable or sufficiently grounded if called upon to assist others.

SELF-DEVELOPMENT LESSON Insight comes from within, and it is important to remain open to receiving inspiration from a deeper source. Nevertheless, you also need to be discerning, so that you do not become distracted by unrealistic desires.

WORKBOOK EXERCISES

1. Record three times in your life when you allowed daydreams or fantasies to get in the way of everyday practical reality.
2. What were the outcomes? How would you respond to these situations now?

KING OF CUPS

DESCRIPTION The King's throne is robust and stable even though it floats on a turbulent sea. Attired in a long robe, the King holds a large cup in his right hand and a short scepter in his left. Around his neck he wears a golden chain bearing the emblem of a fish. A ship is visible in the distance on the right, and on the left a dolphin leaps from the waves. *Element: Air of Water*

INTERPRETATION The King of Cups is a fair and just ruler, well versed in business, law, and divinity. His calm exterior disguises his emotional nature. He takes full responsibility for his actions. Drawing this card indicates that you, too, have reached a level of emotional maturity and stability, and you act with discipline rather than on impulse. You are willing to downplay your emotions in order to assist others.

REVERSE MEANING You may be involved in scandal, double-dealing, or some other form of dishonest or deceptive behavior. There is a distinct possibility that you may face considerable loss.

SELF-DEVELOPMENT LESSON You need to eliminate outmoded ways of thinking and develop your self-knowledge. Once we have mastered our emotions, we are capable of sound judgement.

WORKBOOK EXERCISES

1. Have you always acted fairly when required to make an honest and dispassionate decision? List three occasions when you did act fairly in making a difficult decision.
2. Now list three occasions when you allowed personal friendships or other factors to sway your judgement. How would you act today?

ACE OF SWORDS

DESCRIPTION A hand emerges from clouds holding an upturned sword. The sword is double-edged, and its tip is encircled by a crown. An olive branch, representing peace, and a palm leaf, representing victory, are attached to the crown. Six Yods float above the handle of the sword—the number Six represents balance. *Element: Air*

INTERPRETATION This card represents conquest or triumph. Success is close at hand. You are able to apply both your logic and intuition to clarify matters that concern you, and your anxieties will soon disappear. Nevertheless, if you are involved in a new venture, plan your steps with care and do not act in haste.

REVERSE MEANING You allow excessive power to sway your judgement. You are worried and depressed and expect the worst to happen. You face defeat.

SELF-DEVELOPMENT LESSON The Ace is a double-edged sword, so the challenge here is to explore your personal power holistically and not remain divided. Learn to respond both intellectually and emotionally to the world around you. This involves developing your powers of discrimination so you can reconcile elements that may first appear to you as opposites.

WORKBOOK EXERCISES

1. List three occasions when you acted on your powers of intuition to produce a positive outcome. If you had applied straightforward logic to the same situations, would you have achieved the same result?
2. Which do you value more—intuition or rational logic? Look back at the Tree of Life in Chapter Three. Locate the spheres of awareness that relate to intuition and rational thought.

TWO OF SWORDS

DESCRIPTION A young blindfolded woman sits on a bench. Her arms are crossed and she holds two large swords across her shoulders—one to the left, the other to the right. Jagged rocks emerge from the sea behind her. A new Moon shines down on her. *Element: Air*

INTERPRETATION This card represents an uneasy balance. The young woman is blindfolded and this suggests she is unwilling to face up to certain obstacles that have arisen—the rocks emerging from the waters. However, her posture demonstrates calm detachment and patience. In drawing this card, you sense the need for balance between your rational and intuitive faculties while lacking the courage to break out of the stalemate you have imposed upon yourself. You may be seeking to protect yourself against someone else when in fact no threat exists. This card indicates problems ahead unless you can resolve the question of where you are headed.

REVERSE MEANING Beware of unscrupulous operators. You may feel free to move, but dangers still lurk close at hand. Exercise great care in everything you do.

SELF-DEVELOPMENT LESSON You may be your own worst enemy. Get out of your own way.

WORKBOOK EXERCISES

1. Write down the details of three occasions when difficult decisions you had to make seemed balanced on a knife-edge.
2. What was it that propelled you to act as you did? Would you act differently today?

THREE OF SWORDS

DESCRIPTION A heart pierced by three swords floats in the sky. Dark storm clouds have gathered menacingly in the heavens, and rain is falling. This card is traditionally known as the Lord of Sorrow. *Element: Air*

INTERPRETATION The most basic and obvious interpretation of this card is that it represents a broken heart. Stormy weather lurks ahead in the quest for love, there are conflicts and upheavals in the family, and perhaps lovers will part as the result of a quarrel. The card may also signify more general principles: division, rupture, dispersion, and conflict. However, the card also has a positive side. It urges us to deal honestly in affairs of the heart, to be true and forthright in our relationships, and to avoid manipulating our loved ones emotionally. The Three of Swords also signifies the act of plunging order into chaos, so we are invited here to open our hearts to new insights and perceptions in order to move on from a fixed position or belief system that we have been rigidly holding on to.

REVERSE MEANING Alienation, loss, disorder, and confusion.

SELF-DEVELOPMENT LESSON From pain comes wisdom and understanding. Love is only possible when honesty prevails.

WORKBOOK EXERCISES

1. What have been the three most unhappy events in your life so far?
2. How did you deal with your sense of grief or loss in each situation?
3. How successful are you in finding something positive to hold on to when you seem to be sliding into sadness or despair? List three positive ways of responding to grief.

FOUR OF SWORDS

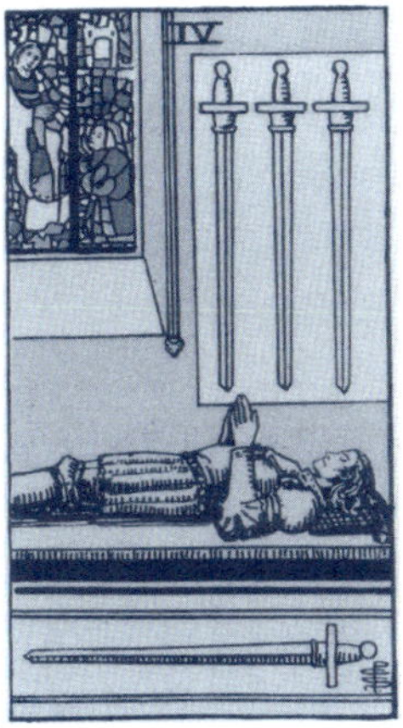

DESCRIPTION This card depicts the effigy of a medieval knight in an attitude of prayer. He lies full-length upon his tomb beneath a traditional stained-glass church window. *Element: Air*

INTERPRETATION Known as the Lord of Rest from Strife, the Four of Swords suggests that the chaos present in the Three of Swords has been redeemed. This card has a calming, introspective quality. In drawing this card, you are invited to explore all the conflicting elements that require resolution in your innermost being. You may also be in need of some form of healing. Another possibility with the Four of Swords is that you have retreated from higher guidance and are in need of spiritual renewal. Your prayer or meditation will open your mind and heart to spiritual insight.

REVERSE MEANING You are active once again. Proceed with caution and summon your powers of discretion.

SELF-DEVELOPMENT LESSON While we may feel more secure within conventional belief systems, opening ourselves to higher spiritual guidance will enable us to move beyond the context of our everyday problems and conflicts.

WORKBOOK EXERCISES

1. Write down three occasions when you allowed positive thoughts or some other form of healing to replace your sense of loss or grief.
2. What advice would you offer others faced with a similar situation? And where do you look for your own spiritual guidance?

FIVE OF SWORDS

DESCRIPTION Storm clouds dominate the heavens. A disdainful man looks back mockingly at two other figures whose swords he has captured. The two defeated figures look distraught. *Element: Air*

INTERPRETATION Known as the Lord of Defeat, this card signifies degradation, destruction, dishonor, failure, and loss. The figure in the foreground is the person in control of the situation, so clearly both conqueror and conquered are shown here. The individual meaning involved in drawing this card will be influenced by the nature of the other cards next to it in the spread. In addition to defeat and loss, cowardice and cruelty could also be elements in the interpretation. On the positive side, there may be an indication here that you need to salvage something worthwhile and enduring from an adverse situation—a lesson can be learned from what has taken place.

REVERSE MEANING You still suffer loss, but it is not as severe as you expected. You win an empty victory. You show deceit in your dealings with others.

SELF-DEVELOPMENT LESSON If you have just emerged victorious from a situation of conflict, what is the cost of your victory? Has it come at the expense of others? If you have been defeated on this occasion, what can you do to ensure that you are not exploited in the future?

WORKBOOK EXERCISES

1. Write down three occasions in your life when you have lost heavily—either financially or in your personal relationships (or both!). Is there anything you could have done to change or avoid these outcomes?
2. How would you respond to a serious loss today? Could anything positive emerge from it? Write down your answers.

SIX OF SWORDS

DESCRIPTION We are shown a ferryman carrying two passengers in his punt across a river to the farther shore. The two passengers are shrouded in shawls, as if in mourning. Six swords, reminiscent in this context of graveyard crosses, are arranged vertically in the prow. *Element: Air*

INTERPRETATION This card combines the symbolism of the number Six—associated with equilibrium, as well as motherhood and marriage—with the Swords, which often indicate strife and misfortune. If you have drawn the Six of Swords, the message is that it is important to move on after setbacks. You are emerging from sorrow and loss; harmony will finally prevail. This journey across water, symbolic of human consciousness, will prove to be a journey of learning and personal development. You will emerge from your difficulties much wiser and in a more balanced frame of mind.

REVERSE MEANING There is no way to escape your present difficulties—you must stay put and see what happens. A journey you have planned will be postponed.

SELF-DEVELOPMENT LESSON This is a journey you have to make. You have the strength and persistence to reach your goal. Set your sights on what you can achieve in the future.

WORKBOOK EXERCISES

1. Write down three situations in your life where you were able to emerge from apparent failure and achieve success.
2. Make a priority list of the ten attributes that you think are important for avoiding failure and achieving success.

SEVEN OF SWORDS

DESCRIPTION A young man is carrying a bundle of swords away from a military camp. This could be a prank, or perhaps he is stealing them. *Element: Air*

INTERPRETATION This card is known as the Lord of Unstable Effort, which clearly warns against hasty, deceitful, or impulsive behavior. The central message of the Seven of Swords seems reasonably clear: Do not take what does not belong to you. Your plans are not working out as you expected and are likely to fail. You are trying to get away with something at someone else's expense. You have betrayed a confidence. You have done something dishonorable and are trying to escape. You are proving unreliable.

REVERSE MEANING You provide reliable advice to another person. You can be trusted. Something that has been stolen from you will be returned.

SELF-DEVELOPMENT LESSON When there are important things to consider, do not allow yourself to be distracted from the main issues at hand. Take time to consider the consequences of your actions. Do not act hastily or on impulse.

WORKBOOK EXERCISES

1. Think of three occasions when you acted rashly or betrayed a confidence. What were the outcomes? Write them down.
2. List five human attributes that you think are crucial to ethical human behavior.

EIGHT OF SWORDS

DESCRIPTION A robed woman stands bound and blindfolded, surrounded by eight swords whose tips have been wedged into the ground; they seem to provide some form of barrier. The earth beneath the woman's feet is soft, wet, and marshy. In the distance is the outline of a castle on a rocky headland. *Element: Air*

INTERPRETATION At present you feel trapped, but your bondage is of your own making and is likely to be short-lived. It may be that, trapped by your own fears, beliefs, and insecurities, you are fearful of moving beyond your present situation. More generally, this card signifies someone who is indecisive, who may be too weak to stand up for himself, or who is trapped in illusory thoughts that become a barrier to personal development. Drawing this card may also indicate that you have been weakened by a temporary illness that is debilitating you and restricting your activities.

REVERSE MEANING You are no longer fearful. You are free from all constraints. You can make a fresh start.

SELF-DEVELOPMENT LESSON At present you are basing your plans on a set of false assumptions, and this will impede your progress. Reconsider the situation, and question why you are proceeding in the manner you have chosen. You will need to explore other options, but make the final decisions yourself rather than being swayed by the opinions of others.

WORKBOOK EXERCISES

1. Write down three occasions in your life when you felt held back by what you believed at the time to be true and later found out was illusory.
2. Write down five positive and five negative things about yourself that you believe are true. What are your strategies for changing the negatives into positives?

NINE OF SWORDS

DESCRIPTION A woman sits weeping in her bed, her cupped hands covering her face in despair. Her bedcover is decorated with motifs from the zodiac, and a woodcut on the side of her bed shows a swordsman vanquishing his opponent in a conflict. *Element: Air*

INTERPRETATION Known as the Lord of Despair and Cruelty, this card signifies suffering, severe doubt, and utter desolation. Although the card is primarily associated with the loss of a loved one through injury or illness, it can also refer to separation in a more general sense. It may also mean that you are taking on the burdens of others, irrespective of whether you are capable of solving their problems or not. In drawing this card, you may also be experiencing a feeling of personal shame, which needs to be acknowledged and resolved.

REVERSE MEANING You have received good news relating to a loved one. The future holds hope and reassurance.

SELF-DEVELOPMENT LESSON If you are feeling sorrowful, you will need to confront the source of your sadness, anger, or shame, because this is holding you back. This is a time for self-appraisal.

WORKBOOK EXERCISES

1. What sorts of doubts do you feel afflicted by? Write down your five worst doubts and misgivings—your most typical responses to negative situations.
2. When you consider these doubts, do you think you have the courage to move beyond them? Make a five-point priority list of ways to respond more positively to doubt or despair in the future.

TEN OF SWORDS

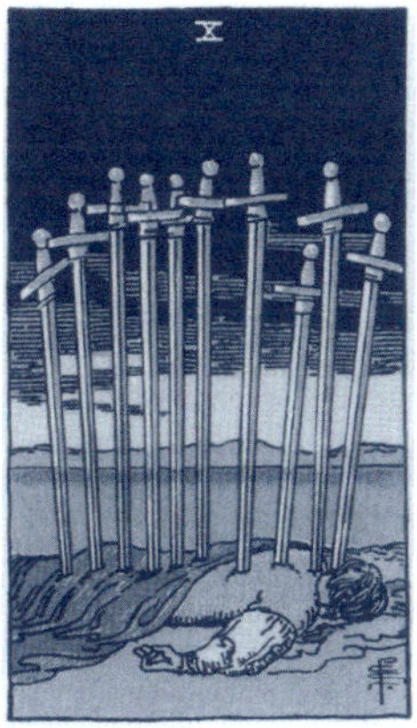

DESCRIPTION A man lies dead on the ground, fatally wounded by ten swords that have been stabbed into his back. The dark and gloomy sky overhead heightens the feeling of tragedy. The fingers of the dead man's right hand are bent over, and touch each other in a ritual gesture suggesting completion. *Element: Air*

INTERPRETATION Although this card seems at first to suggest violent death, it is more about deep and profound loss. If you draw this card, you may well be feeling that all is lost—in your work or in personal relationships. Perhaps the hatred and aggression you are experiencing from other people is overwhelming you, or your business plans have come to nothing. There is also another interpretation that may relate to your personal situation. Perhaps a part of you has just died but you are now opening to something new and inspirational. The number Ten signifies completion, but symbolically death also leads to rebirth. Your lower, ego-driven self has to die so that your higher self can open to spiritual awakening.

REVERSE MEANING Improved health, greater personal success, and prosperity.

SELF-DEVELOPMENT LESSON Endings are also beginnings. This is the close of one chapter in your life and the beginning of a new one. You will have to discard some of your old, outmoded ways of thinking before you can move on.

WORKBOOK EXERCISES

1. What is the worst thing that has ever happened to you, and how did you deal with it?
2. If something like this ever happened again, how would you respond differently? Make a five-point list of ways you might respond in the future to serious loss or tragedy.

PAGE OF SWORDS

DESCRIPTION As mentioned earlier, the Page can be a young man or woman. Here the Page grasps the sword with both hands as if in a heightened state of alertness. The sky above the Page is cloudy, and birds can be seen flying in formation, but we can also see that it is windy because the trees in the distance are bent over to one side. The terrain is rugged and uneven. *Element: Earth of Air*

INTERPRETATION This card signifies authority and vigilance. You are ready for what is coming next, and this sense of confidence and self-assuredness is based on your personal experience. You may be going through a troubled, uneven period in your personal relationships and this will require some form of resolution, but the outlook is basically positive, for any conflicts that you have been experiencing are coming to an end. You don't have to feel defensive. Do not delay your plans. This is a time to move ahead.

REVERSE MEANING Something unexpected could lie ahead, and you will have to deal with it. You may receive news that you regard as disappointing, and this will disrupt your plans for the future.

SELF-DEVELOPMENT LESSON Having passed through a period of doubt and self-evaluation, you are now poised for action. This card signifies that you are prepared to discard past illusions and release yourself from obsessions, and are able to make a fresh start.

WORKBOOK EXERCISES

1. What is your vision for the year ahead? Make a ten-point plan of the things you hope to achieve.

KNIGHT OF SWORDS

DESCRIPTION An armored knight, his visor raised and his helmet plume streaming back in the wind, rides his horse speedily into battle. Storm clouds scatter across the sky, and in the distance cypress trees bend in the gale. The horse's harness is embellished with bird and butterfly motifs. *Element: Fire of Air*

INTERPRETATION This card is known as the Lord of the Winds and Breezes and also as the King of the Spirits of the Air. You are skillful and clever, but also inclined to be impetuous and headstrong. On this occasion you are rushing into a new, untested situation. You are obviously very confident of success—your protective visor is raised and you do not anticipate strong opposition. This card generally signifies bravery, defense, wrath, enmity, and war.

REVERSE MEANING You are a troublemaker and ready to start a fight. You are guarded and secretive about your plans. There is someone you should avoid, as this person may upset your plans and cause havoc.

SELF-DEVELOPMENT LESSON This is a time to recognize and confront destructive aspects in your personal life and relationships. Be patient, and wait a little longer before proceeding.

WORKBOOK EXERCISES

1. Think of three occasions when you rushed into a situation and made a decision you later regretted.
2. How would you act differently today? Make a five-point checklist for avoiding impetuous or rash behavior.

QUEEN OF SWORDS

DESCRIPTION The Queen of Air surveys her realm. In her right hand she holds a sword aloft, and with her left she makes a gesture as if beckoning to her subjects. The Queen looks stern and severe, as if she is repressing her sorrow, but she is not sitting in judgement. Clouds are building up in the sky; a solitary bird flies overhead. In the distance we can see a cluster of cypress trees. The Queen's crown and the base of her throne are decorated with butterflies and a sylph—representing the element Air. *Element: Water of Air*

INTERPRETATION The Queen is perceptive and confident in everything she does, and she is also a good counselor. Nevertheless there is something sad about her, as if she has suffered widowhood or has lost a child. Drawing this card signifies that you are suppressing your emotions and allowing your intellect to rule. You have suffered some sort of grief or a setback, but are now in the process of transforming this negative experience into something far more positive.

REVERSE MEANING You are inclined to be deceptive in your actions. You have good insights into human nature, but you draw on your perceptions to harm other people.

SELF-DEVELOPMENT LESSON You are seeking to transform grief into wisdom, but in doing this you are allowing your intellect to override your emotions. In your approach to everyday life, you should allow room for your intuition to express itself.

WORKBOOK EXERCISES

1. Write down the five things that you think are the most important in developing a greater sense of confidence.
2. How would you rate yourself at present? Write down a five-point checklist for achieving greater personal confidence.

KING OF SWORDS

DESCRIPTION The King sits facing us upon his throne, as if in stern judgement. In his right hand he holds an upturned sword. Storm clouds are building in the sky, and two birds are flying away. Cypress trees are visible in the distance. *Element: Air of Air*

INTERPRETATION The King of Swords has very obvious authority. He has the power to command, but he is also cautious and somewhat suspicious of those who come before him. The King thinks carefully before committing himself to a particular viewpoint. This is a card relating to matters of judgement and legal counsel. In drawing it, you are reminded that, while both your intellectual and intuitive powers are at their peak at the moment, you must continue to draw on both faculties jointly if you are to exercise sound judgement.

REVERSE MEANING Evil intentions are indicated. You may encounter someone who is malicious, or you may become entangled in a damaging lawsuit. A judgement is made against you that does not seem fair.

SELF-DEVELOPMENT LESSON You accept your own wise counsel and are ready to do what needs to be done. If you are entering into a new relationship, be sure that your new partner has interests that complement your own.

WORKBOOK EXERCISES

1. List three occasions when you trusted your own judgement ahead of the advice given by others. Were you subsequently justified in the actions you took?
2. List the five most important things that, in your opinion, contribute to sound judgement.

ACE OF PENTACLES

DESCRIPTION As with the other Aces in the deck, a hand comes forth from the clouds—this time offering a single disk or pentacle. The pentacle bears the emblem of the pentagram, a five-pointed star with the tip facing upward. Below the hand we are shown a cottage garden, well cared for, with abundant flowers and an attractive hedge. *Element: Earth*

INTERPRETATION The Ace of Pentacles signifies the beginning of a cycle of prosperity and successful undertakings. More generally, it also represents contentment and personal accomplishment. This is a time when you will begin to taste the fruits of your efforts. You may receive good news, or praise from a friend, and you may even receive an inheritance. This card indicates that you are about to experience considerable happiness and benefit from the good things in life—for you are manifesting prosperity.

REVERSE MEANING Your wealth is making you more miserable or unhappy. Your plans do not materialize. You have a false sense of security. Things do not go your way.

SELF-DEVELOPMENT LESSON This is a new beginning—a time in your life when you can face the future optimistically with a clear vision. Your personal life is stable and fulfilling, and you can expect your business undertakings to prosper.

WORKBOOK EXERCISES

1. List your ten greatest achievements.
2. Do material achievements give you the most pleasure or do you derive equal satisfaction from less specific achievements, like positive relationships with friends and family?
3. Make a priority list of ten ways you think you can achieve happiness and prosperity.

TWO OF PENTACLES

DESCRIPTION We are shown a young man in decorative attire, dancing. He holds two pentacles, connected by a cord that crosses over, forming the sign of infinity. In the distance ships battle against high seas, trying valiantly to stay afloat. *Element: Earth*

INTERPRETATION This young man seems to be caught between two options, and he is trying to make a decision. The sea is turbulent; his emotions are in a state of flux. Nevertheless, he seems able to balance the different forces affecting his life, and his dance indicates that he is treating the situation lightheartedly and not allowing his indecision to weigh him down. If you draw this card, you may find it difficult to get new projects off the ground, but do persist. It would be helpful if you could be more decisive in your approach.

REVERSE MEANING Too much is going on in your life—you have too many irons in the fire. You will receive bad news. Your plans will founder.

SELF-DEVELOPMENT LESSON Look for equilibrium in your life. You have a seemingly infinite capacity to balance several things at once, but your life could easily become topsy-turvy. Try to be more focused.

WORKBOOK EXERCISES

1. List five occasions when you could have acted more decisively to gain a positive outcome.
2. What were the factors that held you back at the time? Write them down. How would you respond differently in the future?
3. Make a five-point checklist relating to decisive future actions.

THREE OF PENTACLES

DESCRIPTION A stonemason is carving a design on the wall of a medieval monastery or church. Three pentacles form part of the central architectural design. The stonemason is turning to converse with a monk and another hooded figure, who may be a nun. They seem to be engaged in a cooperative and constructive discussion about the work at hand. *Element: Earth*

INTERPRETATION You have considerable creative ability and your work is now being recognized, earning high praise. This card signifies that your efforts are producing great material success. You are likely to receive a financial reward or other form of recognition.

REVERSE MEANING Your work is mediocre and could definitely be improved. You are too inexperienced—you need to learn more. You are more concerned with financial rewards than the quality of your work.

SELF-DEVELOPMENT LESSON Body, mind, and spirit are in unison here. You have mastered the skills you require and can move ahead with the knowledge that your state of personal equilibrium will help you achieve your goals. Also, continue to place your trust in the value of teamwork and cooperation.

WORKBOOK EXERCISES

1. We all appreciate some form of recognition for our positive actions and achievements. Make a list of five things you have achieved that you believe are worthy of recognition.
2. Now ask a close friend to list five things about you that they think are worthy of recognition. How do the lists compare?

FOUR OF PENTACLES

DESCRIPTION A crowned figure sits on a small bench grasping a pentacle to his chest. This figure has apparently come from the city that is visible in the distance, and he seems to be doing everything possible to retain his possessions. He seems cautious and distrustful, as if he is jealously guarding the fruits of his labor. *Element: Earth*

INTERPRETATION Drawing this card signifies that you are overly concerned with material success and physical possessions. You may also be turning your back on the community that has provided you with opportunities to accumulate your wealth. Hanging on to what you have provides you with a feeling of security, but at the same time you are running the risk of becoming a miserable, ungenerous person. Nevertheless you are focused and determined, with clear-cut goals and sound judgement in your business transactions.

REVERSE MEANING You are confronted with major loss or serious obstacles. Another reverse meaning: You are too free with your money, and will need to call a halt to unnecessary spending.

SELF-DEVELOPMENT LESSON If you draw this card, you may well be turning your back on your friends and colleagues and closing yourself off from new ideas and creative input. You will need to open your heart and your mind and heed the advice of those who can help you.

WORKBOOK EXERCISES

1. Make a prioritized list of the ten things that you think are the most important in your life.
2. How many of these are material things? How many of your listings relate to people and relationships—to friends and family?
3. Does your list equate with the personal values you believe in?

FIVE OF PENTACLES

DESCRIPTION Two beggars are making their way through a snowstorm. They pass a church window with five pentacles in its stained-glass design. One beggar huddles in a shawl to stay warm; the other is walking on crutches. *Element: Earth*

INTERPRETATION Drawing this card—which is traditionally known as the Lord of Material Trouble—signifies that you need to review your life in order to establish for yourself what you want to achieve and how you can go about this. Your health and good fortune have deserted you; you may also be losing your way both spiritually and physically. You are not looking after yourself adequately, your life is in disarray, and love seems far away. You have entered "the dark night of the soul"—everything seems aligned against you.

REVERSE MEANING You accept the lessons of life even when they are adverse, and try to overcome the obstacles you are facing. You may be offered a new job. A new sense of spiritual awakening enriches your life.

SELF-DEVELOPMENT LESSON You can use your present afflictions as an opportunity for personal growth. You may be feeling emotionally wounded or spiritually empty, but you have now come to a turning point. Whether you go forward in a more positive light will be entirely up to you.

WORKBOOK EXERCISES

1. As things are now, what are the five most serious issues or concerns that stand in the way of the success you hope to achieve in the coming year? Write them down.
2. Now grade these issues or concerns by level of importance. Create a five-point strategy for facing the challenges that lie ahead and meeting them head-on.

SIX OF PENTACLES

DESCRIPTION A wealthy merchant stands holding a pair of scales, weighing money so he can distribute it fairly to the needy and homeless. Two such figures kneel before him, catching the coins as the merchant drops them into their waiting hands. *Element: Earth*

INTERPRETATION This card draws our attention to the act of sharing our prosperity with others. In drawing the Six of Pentacles, you can expect to receive what is rightfully yours, and you will enjoy the results of your labors. The card is also generally associated with charity, gifts, and philanthropy, and may indicate that a bonus or promotion is possible at work. According to folk legend, "The bread thrown upon the waters of Life will come back threefold," and that is very much the implied meaning here.

REVERSE MEANING You find yourself in an adverse financial or business situation. You receive gifts, but they are given as a bribe. Your present state of prosperity is threatened by jealousy or unethical behavior.

SELF-DEVELOPMENT LESSON You may wish to ask yourself whether you are being as generous to others as you could be, and also whether you are being fair to yourself. You may need to be kinder to those around you and also pay more attention to those aspects of yourself that require greater care and consideration.

WORKBOOK EXERCISES

1. List five indulgences that you have given yourself in the past year.
2. Now list the occasions in the same period when you have been equally generous to others. Which list is longer? (This may speak for itself.)

SEVEN OF PENTACLES

DESCRIPTION A young man leans thoughtfully on his hoe, reflecting on the produce that is growing in his field. *Element: Earth*

INTERPRETATION This card is known as the Lord of Success Unfulfilled, indicating that everything is not going as well as it could. A lot of hard work has already gone into planting and caring for the crop, and part of the meaning here is evaluating the consequences of that hard work. However, a sense of hesitancy also prevails. If you draw this card, prepare yourself for the fact that your expectations may be unfulfilled, at least in the short term. One of the other keys to this card, however, is patience. If you are involved in complicated business transactions, take time to reflect on the likely outcome—this is not the time for rash decision making. The Seven of Pentacles indicates that there is still further work to do if you are to achieve a satisfactory outcome.

REVERSE MEANING Impatience, anxiety, and depression. Your investments will prove to be unprofitable.

SELF-DEVELOPMENT LESSON Pause and take stock of the situation, but then be willing to persevere. If you are patient, you are more likely to achieve success.

WORKBOOK EXERCISES

1. List ten things you are hoping to achieve in the year ahead. Is anything likely to get in the way and prevent your success?
2. Make a ten-point list for identifying possible obstacles to your personal achievements and create a strategy for dealing with these obstacles, one by one.

EIGHT OF PENTACLES

DESCRIPTION A young stonemason—possibly an apprentice—is busy at work, carving the form of the pentagram on one of the pentacles. Another completed pentacle lies on the ground, and six others are displayed like trophies in a vertical presentation. *Element: Earth*

INTERPRETATION Known as the Lord of Prudence, the Eight of Pentacles is associated with work, employment, craftsmanship, and dedication to a particular task. It may also indicate that some small remuneration is on the way. This stonemason is young and inexperienced compared to the artisan depicted on the Three of Pentacles—who is shown sculpting a motif on a church or monastery wall—but nevertheless he shows considerable dedication at developing and refining his skills. If you draw this card, there is a clear indication that you are learning a new skill, trade, or profession, and, while you may not yet be receiving substantial monetary reward for your efforts, you are definitely on the right track. However, it may also indicate that you are so absorbed in your work that you are neglecting your relationships.

REVERSE MEANING You need clear directives and guidance. You are going about things the wrong way. You avoid hard work. You are using your skills for unethical ends.

SELF-DEVELOPMENT LESSON You have considerable talents and potential, but you can refine and develop these talents still further with perseverance and discipline.

WORKBOOK EXERCISES

1. What new skills would you like to acquire in the year ahead? Write them down.
2. Now prioritize them and make a ten-point plan for acquiring these skills, allowing a sensible amount of time for each skill to guarantee success.

NINE OF PENTACLES

DESCRIPTION An elegant, handsomely attired woman stands alone in a vineyard. She is wealthy, the vineyard is part of her estate, and her manor house is visible in the background. A falcon rests on her gloved left hand. *Element: Earth*

INTERPRETATION Drawing this card signifies that you have achieved financial success and satisfaction through a high level of personal accomplishment. You are quite at home in your own company, and you are enjoying the good things in life. Nevertheless, your self-confidence and independence may be making you somewhat aloof and a little self-centered, so there could be room here to develop your relationships with those around you.

REVERSE MEANING Possible loss of friends or one's own home. Legal difficulties. This is a time to reconsider your goals and personal desires.

SELF-DEVELOPMENT LESSON You have reached a peak in terms of self-reliance and material success. However, the Nine of Pentacles is known as the Lord of Material Gain, so steady progress still needs to be made in the areas of emotional and spiritual growth.

WORKBOOK EXERCISES

1. Think of five occasions in the past year when you have allowed your preoccupation with work or busy schedules to get in the way of catching up with friends or family.
2. Make a list of the friends or family you want to see soon. Book a time for a get-together with the special people in your life.

TEN OF PENTACLES

DESCRIPTION The patriarch sits with two dogs at his feet. His coat of arms is on a nearby archway. Nearby, two other members of the family—a young man and woman—talk cheerfully to each other. The scene is one of clan or family solidarity, built on many years of tradition. Ten pentacles are superimposed on this medieval family setting, and are aligned according to the spheres of the Kabbalistic Tree of Life. *Element: Earth*

INTERPRETATION On one level this card symbolizes material prosperity, prestige, and family stability. If you draw this card, you can be assured of financial prosperity and security in your personal affairs, and you may also enjoy newfound recognition in your chosen field of endeavor. However, the presence of the ten pentacles in the form of the Tree of Life (see the diagram on page 41) reminds us that we are members of both an individual family and a community of spiritual seekers. It is important that in our everyday lives we strive not only for physical well-being and prosperity, but also for spiritual fulfillment. The Ten of Pentacles signifies that lasting prosperity is grounded in spiritual wisdom and understanding.

REVERSE MEANING Family misfortunes. Loss of honor or prestige.

SELF-DEVELOPMENT LESSON Having achieved success in material terms, the quest is now to experience the higher spiritual realms. This card represents both the culmination of our present worldly existence and an opening to new dimensions of spiritual awareness.

WORKBOOK EXERCISES

1. You may be enjoying material success, but what about spiritual riches? List five ways in which you could open yourself more completely to the spiritual realm.
2. Make a five-point checklist for acting on these approaches soon.

PAGE OF PENTACLES

DESCRIPTION A youthful figure stands in a field of flowers holding a pentacle in his raised hands. The Page is staring intently at the pentacle, which seems almost to be hovering in the air. *Element: Earth of Earth*

INTERPRETATION The Page of Pentacles signifies diligence and thoughtfulness, as well as study and scholarship. If you draw this card, you can expect good news that is likely to have a significant impact on your everyday life. You may also experience changes for the better through the efforts of someone who cares for you, or you may meet someone who is kind and sympathetic to your point of view. This card generally signifies an openness to new ideas and a warm, caring disposition.

REVERSE MEANING You will receive unfavorable news. You become rebellious and moody. You find yourself surrounded by people who hold opinions quite different from your own.

SELF-DEVELOPMENT LESSON You may be so focused at the present on your own pursuits that you have become insensitive to the needs of others. Look to a future that is not only a positive one for you, but also extends beyond your personal horizons.

WORKBOOK EXERCISES

1. List five things that you are hoping to achieve in the year ahead. List them in order of priority.
2. Now take time to reflect on that list. Is it realistic? Establish a five-point list for achieving your goals and building a positive future.

KNIGHT OF PENTACLES

DESCRIPTION An armored knight is shown riding a sturdy, slow-moving horse. He wears a sprig of green on his helmet and looks thoughtfully at the pentacle that he holds in his cupped hands. Gentle rolling hills are visible in the distance. *Element: Fire of Earth*

INTERPRETATION This card signifies endurance and consistency rather than passion. This knight is certainly trustworthy and reliable, but he lacks imagination and proceeds at a slow, plodding pace. If you draw this card, it is likely that you embody many of these qualities and are steady rather than spectacular in your path through life.

REVERSE MEANING Inertia, idleness, carelessness, and impatience. Business and financial affairs are at a standstill.

SELF-DEVELOPMENT LESSON You are good at getting things done, but sometimes you forget to connect with the everyday pleasures of life. This card is a call to reawaken your dormant passionate self.

WORKBOOK EXERCISES

1. Write down five qualities relating to passion, imagination, or creativity that are missing from your life at present.
2. Make a ten-point priority plan to allow time to bring these qualities into your life in the year ahead.

QUEEN OF PENTACLES

DESCRIPTION The dark-haired Queen of Fertility sits on her throne holding a pentacle lovingly in her lap. Around her, Nature is abundant. A bower of roses arches above her, a rabbit nibbles grass at her feet, and a lush wooded valley is visible in the distance. The back of the Queen's throne is decorated with a Cupid and fruit motifs. *Element: Water of Earth*

INTERPRETATION The Queen of the Thrones of Earth is a creative and intelligent woman, well versed in the ways of the world. She is charitable, thoughtful, and mature, and applies her creativity in matters associated with both family and business. Drawing this card signifies that you, too, have these positive qualities. If there is a downside indicated in this card, it is a tendency toward melancholy and moodiness, but you are always willing to assist others in need, so your moodiness is unlikely to last very long.

REVERSE MEANING You depend too much on other people. You are neglecting your duties. You are mistrustful and suspicious. Your creative abilities are not being developed.

SELF-DEVELOPMENT LESSON You are ever willing to serve others, but sometimes your contribution and dedication are taken for granted. Take care to attend to your personal needs as well, and focus on your priorities.

WORKBOOK EXERCISES

1. List three occasions in recent times when you felt someone had taken advantage of you. How did you respond on those occasions and how do you feel about them now?
2. Make a five-point list of positive affirmations to enable you to stand up for yourself in the period that lies ahead.

KING OF PENTACLES

DESCRIPTION The King of Pentacles sits on his throne amid all the signs of wealth, power, and authority. He holds a scepter in his right hand and a pentacle in his left. His throne is decorated with bulls' heads, and his robe with clusters of grapes and vine leaves. The turrets of his castle are visible. *Element: Air of Earth*

INTERPRETATION In a modern context, we would describe the King of Pentacles as a captain of industry. He has considerable executive power and lucid intelligence, and is skilled in mathematics. He is consistent and reliable, has great financial expertise, and is courageous in the face of adversity. If you have drawn this card, you embody many of these qualities.

REVERSE MEANING You have become too materialistic. You are shallow and opinionated and often appear stupid in the eyes of others. You are vulnerable to bribes. You are using your talents in unethical ways.

SELF-DEVELOPMENT LESSON You are successful and reliable, but at times you are so involved in business matters that your close personal relationships suffer. The lesson here is to balance the needs of friends and family with your innate capacity to manage your business and financial concerns successfully.

WORKBOOK EXERCISES

1. Who are the ten most important people in your everyday life? Write down their names.
2. Have you neglected any of these people by placing your business and financial affairs ahead of your close personal ties?
3. Make a checklist of close friends you need to catch up with soon.

CHAPTER SIX

CLASSIC TAROT SPREADS

Using Tarot spreads to help the seeker: How do I set up the Celtic Cross and Gypsy Spreads? What can I learn from these spreads?

There are several classical Tarot spreads, as well as a large number of variations suggested by contemporary Tarot practitioners. Two of the most popular and well-proven spreads are the **Celtic Cross** (the most classical), and the ***Gypsy Spread***. We will consider a couple of other variations in Chapters Seven and Eight.

THE CELTIC CROSS SPREAD

PREPARING THE CARDS

1. The cards should first be thoroughly shuffled. Approximately half should be in a reverse position so that they really are completely mixed (as you can see from the descriptions in Chapters Four and Five, each card has a reverse aspect, and for balance this needs to be represented in dealing the spread). Both the reader and the seeker should shuffle the cards at the beginning.
2. Now choose a Court card from the deck as a Significator (the criteria for making this choice were outlined in Chapter Three). Place this card faceup in the center of the table.
3. The seeker should then have his or her question firmly in mind while shuffling the cards once again. Typically the questions will fall into one of the following categories:

- Love, marriage, family situations, personal relationships
- Financial and business affairs, property issues
- Career and personal accomplishment, prospects for travel
- Current state of mind, psychic and spiritual issues

4. While the seeker is shuffling the cards and focusing on the question for the reading, the reader should be asking silently for spiritual guidance to assist in providing a valid interpretation of the cards. It may also be helpful for the seeker to state out loud the question for which the reading is being performed. However, if the seeker wishes to keep the question private at this point, it can become part of the discussion after the reading has been done.

LAYING OUT THE CARDS

1. After the seeker has finished shuffling the cards, they should be placed facedown on the table.
2. With the left hand, the seeker should then cut them into three piles and place them on the left.
3. The reader should then pick up the piles one at a time with his or her left hand and in the same sequence as they were laid—pile one first, then pile two, and finally pile three. They are then ready to be laid out in format.

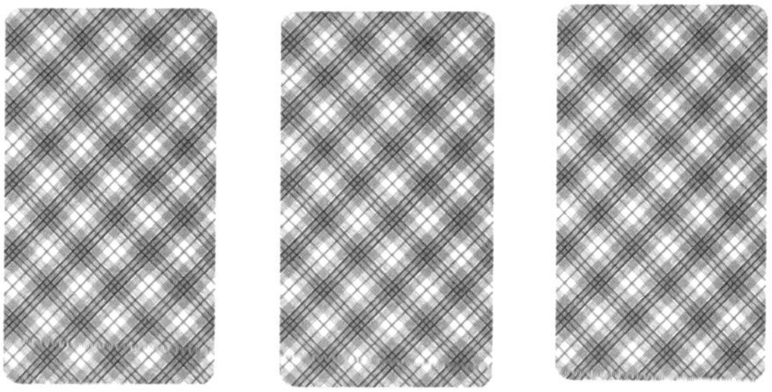

The three piles should be placed facedown by the seeker before being laid out by the reader.

EXPLAINING THE CELTIC CROSS SPREAD

The Celtic Cross is a ten-card "cross and staff" format. See the diagram below. All cards are placed faceup during the reading itself.

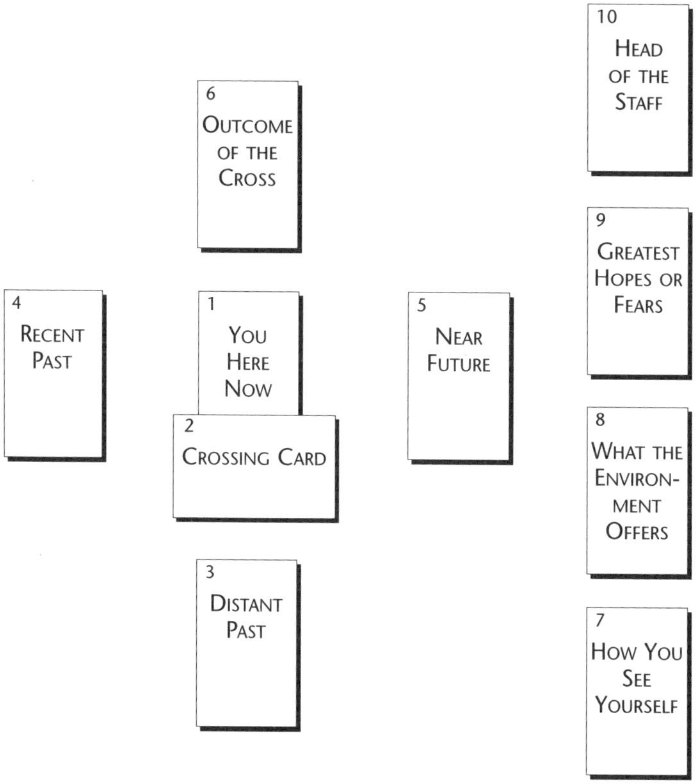

1. The Significator is already in position in the center of the table—this is **Card 1**. Card 1 indicates the seeker's present position, and reflects the influences relating to the question that has been asked silently or out loud. The essential message of Card 1 is: "*Where am I?*"
2. The reader should now take the top card from the pack and place it sideways on top of the Significator—this is known as the ***crossing card***. The top of the card's design should face to the left, the bottom to the right. This is **Card 2** and it represents the immediate influence on the seeker's circumstances. The essential message of Card 2 is: "*What's in my way?*" Some Tarot readers believe that the microcross of Cards 1 and 2 provides the essence of the reading, and that the other cards in the spread spell out the basic message in further detail.
3. **Card 3** is placed in a vertical position directly below Card 2. This represents the distant past and refers to the actual basis of the current concern or the issue at hand—it may relate to something that happened some time ago but has now become a part of the seeker's central life experience. The essential message of Card 3 is: "*Where have I been?*"
4. **Card 4** is placed to the left of Cards 1 and 2. This represents the seeker's recent past and reflects a recent influence or experience. The essential message of Card 4 is: "*What's been happening?*"
5. **Card 5** is placed on the right of Cards 1 and 2 and represents the seeker's near future. This refers to something that may happen soon. The essential message of Card 5 is: "*What's in store for me?*"
6. **Card 6** is placed directly above Card 1 and represents the outcome of the cross. This refers to events that will happen to the seeker in the future, and could include such things as meetings with other people, possible outcomes, influences, choices, etc. The essential message of Card 6 is: "*What are my options?*" Once Card 6 has been laid, the basic cross is complete. The four remaining cards are laid out in a vertical format to the right of the cross, and are known collectively as the ***staff***.
7. **Card 7** is the first card in this vertical formation and it is placed in the lowest position on the staff (see diagram). This card identifies how you see yourself, and refers to the

seeker's present personal concerns—anxieties, fears, worries—in relation to the question that has been asked. The essential message of Card 7 is: "*Who do I think I am?*"

8. **Card 8** is placed in the second lowest position in the vertical formation (see diagram) and refers to what the environment offers. This relates to the opinions and influences of family and friends relating to the question that has been asked. The essential message of Card 8 is: "*What's out there for me?*"
9. **Card 9** is placed in the second highest position in the vertical formation (see diagram), and refers to the seeker's greatest hopes or fears in relation to the question that has been asked. The essential message of Card 9 is: "*What do I expect?*"
10. **Card 10** is placed at the head of the vertical formation (see diagram), and completes the staff. It is known as the head of the staff and represents the final outcome. The essential message of Card 10 is: "*Where does this all lead?*"

SOME INDICATORS FOR THE CELTIC CROSS

When a spread is interpreted, it is generally assumed that the Major Arcana exert the strongest influence on the outcome, followed by the Court cards, and then the "pip" cards of the four suits. If a spread includes three or four cards from the Major Arcana, this can be taken to mean that powerful forces are shaping the destiny of the seeker and that the likely outcome may be beyond his or her control.

We may interpret the presence of multiple cards of the same suit in a spread as follows:

- **Wands** Four or more are an indication of growth, vitality, and positive energy.
- **Cups** Four or more are an indication that there is a strong connection with the emotions—relating especially to love, happiness, family, friends, and children.
- **Swords** Four or more are an indication of very aggressive ambition and possibly of acts of destruction.

- **Pentacles** Four or more refer to issues relating to money, business transactions, or material prosperity.
- **Kings** Two of any suit represent a conference or meeting.
- **Queens** Two of any suit represent gossip and rumor.
- **Knights** Two of any suit represent conflict.
- **Pages** Two of any suit represent happy and playful activities.

WORKBOOK EXERCISES

1. Deal a Celtic Cross Spread and compare the cards that refer to the *past* (Cards 3, 4, and 7) with those that refer to the *present* (Cards 1, 2, and 8) and the *future* (Cards 5, 6, 9, and 10). What additional insights do you gain when you read and analyze the cards in this way?
2. Now consider the spread in terms of what the cards are telling you about the seeker's *aspirations* (Cards 1, 3, and 5), *actions* (Cards 2, 4, and 6), and finally *interactions* (Cards 7, 8, and 9). Responding to the cards in this way should assist your interpretation of the spread.

THE GYPSY SPREAD

PREPARING THE CARDS

1. The reader removes the Major Arcana cards from the pack and then passes the fifty-six cards of the Minor Arcana to the seeker.
2. The seeker then shuffles these cards and separates the first twenty into a pile, placing them facedown on the table. These twenty cards are then combined with the twenty-two Major Arcana cards that were removed. The remaining thirty-six cards are set aside.
3. The seeker now shuffles the forty-two-card pack and lays out the cards one by one, facedown, in six piles of seven cards, from right to left. The first seven cards drawn make up the first pile, the next seven the second pile, and so on.
4. The seeker now picks up each pile in turn, beginning with the first, and deals out the cards, faceup, and working from right to left to produce six rows of seven cards. This creates the six-row Gypsy Spread. The rows number one to six from top to bottom.

WHAT THE GYPSY SPREAD ROWS SIGNIFY

1. **Row 1:** *Past Influences*, which include all those previous influences and past experiences that continue to have an impact on the everyday life of the seeker.
2. **Row 2:** *Present Influences*, which include all influences and current events impacting the seeker at the present time.
3. **Row 3:** *Outside Influences*, which include external social and environmental factors occurring at the present time, and over which the seeker is unable to exert any control.
4. **Row 4:** *Immediate Future Influences*, which include events and influences that are about to impact the life of the seeker. Some of these events may be entirely unexpected.
5. **Row 5:** *Possibilities for the Future*, which include circumstances and events that could occur in the future. However, the seeker has some control over these events and can either welcome them or seek to avoid them—depending on their likely impact.
6. **Row 6:** *Future Results and Outcome*, which include those circumstances and events that will have a distinct and noticeable impact on the future of the seeker.

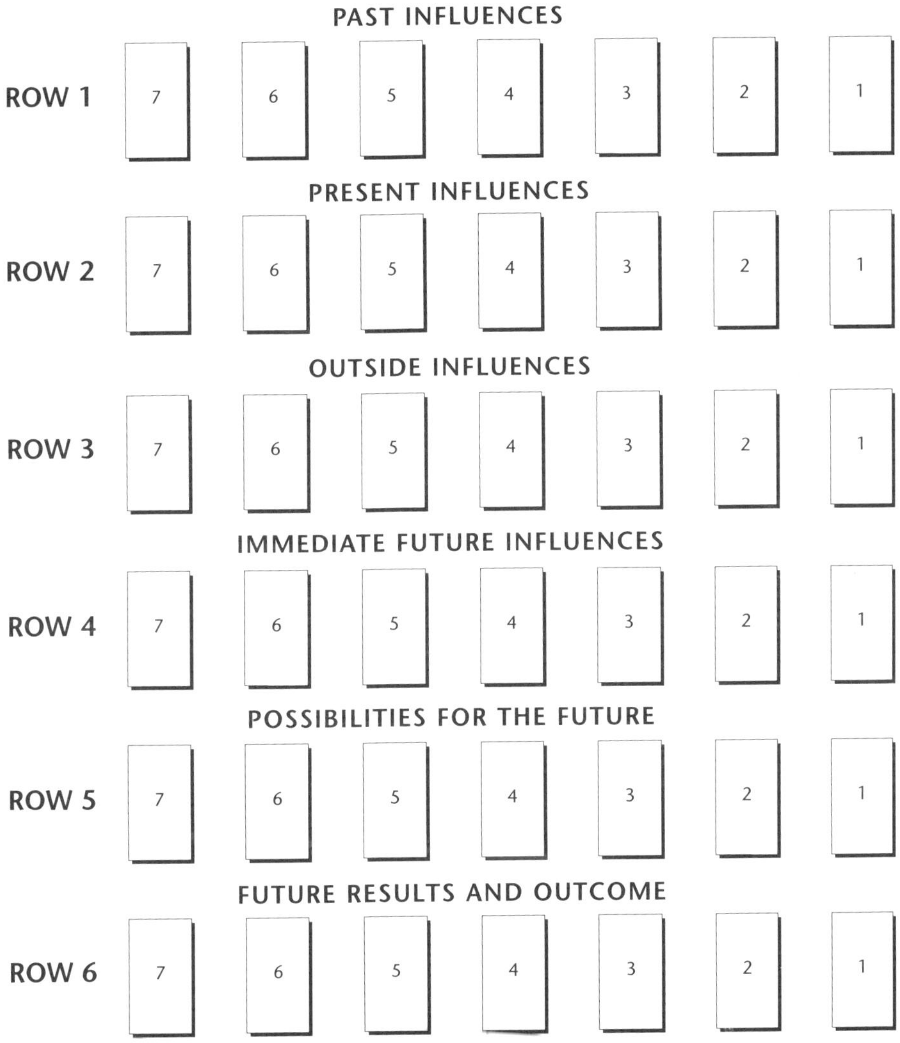

The Gypsy Spread

CHOOSING THE SIGNIFICATOR

In the Gypsy Spread, the method used to choose the Significator is different from that used in the Celtic Cross. Here, if the seeker is male, he can select either the Magician or the Emperor to represent himself, and a female seeker can choose either the High Priestess or the Empress. The Significator is not removed from the pack until all forty-two cards are laid out in the six-row format. Because there are forty-two cards and all the Major Arcana are used in the spread, the Significator will be included in one of the rows. The seeker should now remove it, place the Significator somewhere to the right of the top row, away on its own, and then select a card at random from the other thirty-six cards to replace it in the spread.

The spread can now be interpreted by the reader, who will respond to the cards in a sequence from right to left, beginning with Card 1 in the top row and finishing with Card 7 in the bottom row. This spread is intended to tell the ongoing story of the seeker's past, present, and future, and does not focus on a specific question. For the best results, the reader should take into account the relationship of the cards to each other within the spread, rather than just focusing on one card at a time.

In the Gypsy Spread, the male seeker selects either the Magician or the Emperor as his Significator.

The female seeker selects either the High Priestess or the Empress as her Significator.

GENERAL HINTS FOR INTERPRETING A SPREAD

Reading the cards in a Tarot spread is a bit like reading a book. Although you read a book one page at a time, it is vital to consider the conceptual flow of the text as a whole. In the same way, when you interpret a particular Tarot spread, it is important to look at how the cards relate to one another and to consider them as part of a total presentation. If you neglect to do this, you run the risk that your interpretation of the cards may become disjointed or fragmented, focusing too much on the individual meanings of each card rather than on the message of the spread as a whole.

For this reason it is always a good idea to review the entire spread and try to get some sense of its overall energy flow. Does the spread seem to be heading up or down—is it optimistic and positive, or negative in tendency? Does the future look hopeful or problematic? If there are key issues to be resolved, what is the real nature of their source? Is the spread dominated by the Major Arcana or Court cards? (Four or more Major Arcana or Court cards in a spread will usually prove significant, and may indicate an outcome beyond the seeker's sphere of influence.) If the spread is dominated by seven or more Minor Arcana numbered cards (i.e., Ace to Ten), this indicates that the outcome of the spread can be personally influenced by the seeker.

WORKBOOK EXERCISES

1. Do you have a personal preference for either the Celtic Cross Spread or the Gypsy Spread? Why?
2. Which of these spreads provides deeper insights into any questions you may have about personal relationships? Why do you think that is so?
3. Are you happy with the method used in the Gypsy Spread for selecting the Significator? If not, spend more time with the Celtic Cross approach. Do you find this allows for greater flexibility and individual response to the spreads?
4. Are you remembering to review the spreads as a whole, as well as focusing on the meaning of individual cards?

CHAPTER SEVEN

PERSONAL TAROT SPREADS

Doing a spread for yourself: How do I use the Intuitive technique, the Three Aces Spread, and the Seven Card Spread to seek a response to questions I need answered? What will I learn?

We have explored Tarot readings used to interpret a spread for someone else. However, you may also want to do a spread for yourself, taking the role of seeker. You may be seeking a response to a specific question, or insight in relation to a course of action. You will be seeking guidance from the deepest part of yourself. The Tarot spread will give you an answer—perhaps just "yes" or "no." In the first two approaches described below, you can do everything on your own, while in the Seven Card Spread you will have to ask a friend to deal the cards for you while you seek a response to your question.

There are three different methods for seeking a quick "yes" or "no" response: the Three Aces Spread, the Intuitive technique, and the Seven Card Spread. You may have to try each in turn to see which you like best.

THE THREE ACES SPREAD

Earlier in this book, when we explored the symbolism of numbers, you learned that Aces represent beginnings and reflect individual creativity and vitality. This is why the Aces are used in this spread. When using the Three Aces Spread, your questions should be specific.

1. Shuffle and cut the cards, focusing once again on your question as you do so.
2. Deal the cards into a pile, faceup, but do not allow more than thirteen cards to a pile—if thirteen cards have been dealt, start a new pile on the left. You are looking for an Ace, so keep dealing until an Ace appears.

3. When it does, keep this Ace on top of the pile and start dealing a new pile, again on the left, until a second Ace appears. Keep going until you have produced three piles.
4. When you have dealt three piles, some of them will have Aces on top and others may not.
5. If there are no Aces at all in your spread, your question cannot be answered at this time. If one or two piles are dealt without producing an Ace, you will have to wait a while before resolving the issue at hand. If only one Ace is dealt in the three piles, this will contain the answer you are looking for. If more than one of your piles contains an Ace on top, the Ace on the right contains the first part of the answer and the Ace or Aces on the left refer to the final outcome.

INTERPRETING THE THREE ACES SPREAD

Let's say the question was: "Should I accept my brother Tom's offer to become a partner in his business?" And, for example, the three piles of cards produced the following result, reading right to left: *(right) Ace of Cups reversed, (middle) no Ace, (left) Ace of Pentacles.*

READING THE CARDS

The Ace of Cups signifies the beginning of wisdom and understanding, but when it is reversed it indicates that your spiritual potential is unable to manifest because you are too ego-centered and selfish at the present time. As your brother Tom is inviting you to join his business—which will require collaboration—you will have to work through your self-centeredness in order to become a true and effective partner and make the business venture work. The absence of an Ace in the middle pile suggests that there should be a period of waiting before a final decision is made—and in the context of your self-centeredness this is undoubtedly a good thing! However, the Ace of Pentacles in the third pile signifies the beginning of a cycle of prosperity and successful undertakings. In the long run, then, things look very positive indeed.

THE ANSWER THAT EMERGES FROM THIS READING

Yes, tell Tom you would like to join him in the near future as a partner in his business, but be prepared to do some work on yourself first, so you can join his business in a spirit of true cooperation without putting your own needs ahead of the partnership.

THE INTUITIVE TECHNIQUE

You can use this approach to answer such specific questions as: "Should I travel to Paris for my summer holidays?"; "Will the sale of the company be announced tomorrow?"; or "Is this a good time to buy a new car?"

Shuffle your Tarot deck thoroughly while pondering your question. Cut your cards into three piles, combine them into one, and stay focused on your question as you shuffle the cards thoroughly again. Lay out all seventy-eight cards on the table, facedown.

Now, using only your intuition, select three cards spontaneously. Turn them faceup. These three cards are the only ones that count for this reading. The key to the outcome is whether they are right side up. If all three are, your answer is a definite "yes." If two cards are right side up and one is reversed, the answer is qualified: "Yes, probably." (This may not be a clear enough response to act on, however.) If two cards are reversed and only one is right side up, the answer is "probably not." If all three are reversed, the answer is "definitely no!"

THE SEVEN CARD SPREAD

For this spread, ask your friend to separate the Major Arcana from the Minor Arcana and place the cards in two piles. Your friend should then shuffle the cards from the Minor Arcana pile and deal out the top eleven cards, facedown, on top of the pile containing the Major Arcana cards. The other forty-five cards should be put aside.

Because you are taking the role of the seeker, you should shuffle the thirty-three-card pack facedown—this pack contains twenty-two cards from the Major Arcana and eleven cards from the Minor Arcana. State your question out loud. Your friend should then deal out the first seven cards from the pack and place them faceup from right to left.

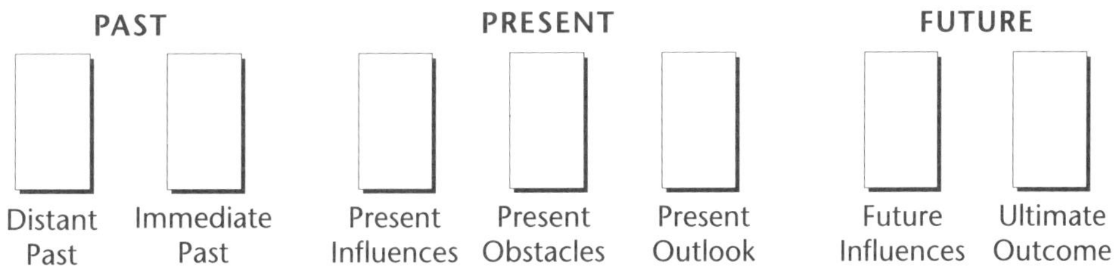

The Seven Card Spread

READING THE CARDS

As you can see from the diagram on page 157, the two cards on the right refer to the future (Future Influences, Ultimate Outcome), the three cards in the center refer to the present (Present Influences, Present Obstacles, Present Outlook), and the two cards on the left refer to the past (Distant Past, Immediate Past). The significance of each of these cards is as follows, and the meanings are explained from the viewpoint of the seeker. In this spread you should read the cards from left to right.

Distant Past This card refers to events and influences that occurred some time ago but have an ongoing effect. These past events are also influencing your current beliefs and opinions.

Immediate Past This card refers specifically to something that has happened recently and that has had a significant effect on you. The impact of this event is only now beginning to recede.

Present Influences This card refers to events and influences occurring right now, and you may notice a connection to the previous card as well. There is also a clear connection with the next two cards in the spread.

Present Obstacles This card refers to dangers and obstacles you are facing right now. If the card you have drawn in this position looks superficially favorable, consider possible ways in which you are being distracted from your main goals.

Present Outlook This card elaborates on the message presented by the two previous cards. It relates to the possible consequences of what you are currently doing and thinking.

Future Influences This card reflects the themes that have emerged in all the previous cards. It indicates the gathering of momentum of all that has accumulated from the past and that will make its presence felt in the near future.

Ultimate Outcome This card represents the culmination of everything that has happened in the past, projected into the future as a likely outcome.

MORE ABOUT THE SEVEN CARD SPREAD

Some points to remember about the Seven Card Spread:

- If four or more cards in your spread are inverted, the answer to your question will probably be "no," or only a very qualified "yes, maybe."
- Inverted cards should be interpreted using their reverse meaning—for details, see card descriptions in Chapters Four and Five.
- Some Tarot practitioners using this spread have suggested that if the first card drawn is inverted, the remaining six should also be inverted to obtain the true meaning of the spread. This is a matter of personal preference—try it both ways and see what works for you!

WORKBOOK EXERCISES

1. How effective is the Intuitive technique for you? Do you really trust your intuition? Think of a time when you have trusted your intuition and acted on it—and everything has worked out fine.
2. Now think of a time when you acted on a hunch and it didn't work out. Why was this so, in your case? Are there issues of trust that you have to resolve? Perhaps this is a good time to try a meditation or relaxation exercise and open your awareness to that inner voice deep within.
3. Try the Three Aces Spread in relation to an important question that is on your mind at the present. How accurate was your reading? Did it provide you with the answer you were seeking?
4. Now try the Seven Card Spread in relation to an important question that is concerning you at the moment. Did you enjoy the role of seeker? Did you feel the cards answered your question? Did the presence of any inverted cards influence your interpretation?

CHAPTER EIGHT

LOVE AND FRIENDSHIP READINGS

Receiving guidance on relationships: How do I use co-reading spreads with my partner? What will I learn from the Three Aces Spread, the Getting to Know You exercise, and Tarot for Two?

The Tarot can also give guidance in a relationship situation. As your relationship with a special friend or a new lover blossoms, you may wish to explore the deep fountain of intuitive wisdom revealed in the Tarot. This may help you see how your love or friendship could develop in the future.

There are two ways of exploring close personal relationships through the Tarot. You can use one of the spreads described in Chapter Seven and relate your individual questions specifically to your friendship or your new love affair, or you and your partner can use a "***co-reading***" approach where you participate jointly in spreading the cards and interpreting them.

USING THE THREE ACES SPREAD

The Three Aces Spread, where you read and interpret on your own, is ideal for simple "yes" and "no" answers. Remember that when you are using this spread, your question should be as specific as possible. Here's how you can apply it to your personal relationships.

As mentioned earlier, Aces represent beginnings, so they are especially relevant to a new relationship that is starting to gather momentum. Aces also reflect our individual creativity and vitality, and will relate to whether the chemistry is right in a relationship.

DOING THE READING

1. Shuffle and cut the cards, focusing once again on your question as you do so.
2. Deal the cards into a pile, faceup, but do not allow more than thirteen cards to a pile—

if thirteen cards have been dealt, start a new pile on the left.

3. You are looking for an Ace, so keep dealing until an Ace appears. When it does, keep this Ace on top of the pile and start dealing a new pile, again on the left, until a second Ace appears.
4. Keep going until you have produced three piles.
5. When you have dealt three piles, some will have Aces on top and others may not. If no Aces at all emerge in your spread, this means that your question cannot be answered at this time. If one or two piles are dealt without containing an Ace, this means that you will have to wait a while before resolving the issue at hand. If only one Ace is dealt in the three piles, it will contain the answer you are looking for. If more than one of your piles contains an Ace on top, the key lies in their position. The Ace on the right contains the first part of the answer, and the Ace or Aces on the left refer to the final outcome. The meanings for each of the Aces are provided in Chapter Five.

INTERPRETING THE THREE ACES SPREAD

Let's say the question was: "Will Jason's busy work commitments get in the way of our new love relationship?" And, again by way of example, let's say the three piles of cards produce the following result, reading from right to left: *(right) Ace of Swords, (middle) Ace of Wands reversed, (left) no Ace*.

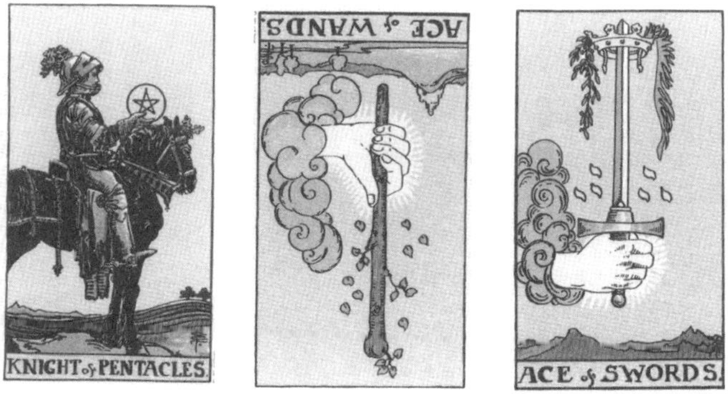

The **Ace of Swords** represents conquest or triumph, which certainly looks positive as an initial response, but this also requires that you apply both intuition and logic to the situation. Your heart may tell you that Jason has already fallen in love with you, but your logic will also remind you that his busy work schedule may get in the way of his emotional commitment to you. He may not have enough time in his life for a deep and enduring love relationship—perhaps his career will come first.

The reversed **Ace of Wands** adds to this insight. The Ace of Wands by itself signifies the beginning of a new venture or relationship, but when reversed it suggests major setbacks along the way. Acts of selfishness or a lack of determination may hinder good things that are happening, and prevent them from flowering into something special.

The lack of an Ace in the third pile of cards suggests that you should certainly hold back from plunging into this relationship too deeply, because you could easily get hurt. The message here is to take it slowly, and not expect too much from this new love affair, because Jason clearly has divided loyalties—to work and to you—and it is by no means obvious at this stage whether his career or his new relationship with you will prove to be more important.

CO-READING

With the Three Aces Spread, you are asking the questions and interpreting the cards on your own—and since you are already involved emotionally in a close personal relationship, you may not find it easy to interpret the cards in a truly balanced way. In such a situation you may find that co-reading the Tarot with your partner is a more satisfactory solution. One of the simplest ways to begin exploring the Tarot of love and friendship through co-reading is to try the following exercise. It will certainly offer insights into both of your personalities, aspirations, and compatibility.

THE GETTING TO KNOW YOU EXERCISE

In this co-reading Tarot exercise, both partners participate equally. Choosing the Significator for the reading means you will have to find a card that suits both of you. As mentioned earlier, the Significator is usually chosen from the Court cards, but on occasion a card from the Major Arcana can also be used. For this purpose, selecting the Lovers may be ideal.

For this co-reading method, you should use the Celtic Cross format described in Chapter Six. To begin the process, place the Significator on the table and then use all of the remaining cards of the Tarot deck. One partner should shuffle the cards until the deck feels right, and then pass it to the other partner, who should then also shuffle it until it feels right. The first partner may then wish to reshuffle, if both agree. One partner should then cut the deck into three stacks with the left hand and restack with the left hand. The other partner can then lay out the spread.

Select a question beforehand that reflects your mutual interests and has a direct bearing on how your relationship currently stands. For example: How successful have we been in combining our hopes and aspirations? What areas of our relationship still require further consolidation and positive effort? What are we hoping for from this relationship? In co-readings, the Tarot cards reflect the relationship itself, rather than the partners as individuals, so bear this in mind when you explore the meaning of each spread.

It is worth remembering that, in readings linked to relationships, few individual spreads will provide conclusive answers to your questions. The reason is that all relationships are built on different levels of connectedness—physical, mental, emotional, sexual, and spiritual—and it is hard to come up with a meaningful question that is specific enough in such a context. One way of dealing with this issue, however, is to develop a range of very focused questions that, taken collectively over a series of readings, will reflect the relationship as a whole. If both partners share in the interpretation of the cards, this can often trigger meaningful insights that will in turn help the relationship to become deeper, richer, and more intimate.

Taking this process further, you might like to explore the unique Double Celtic Cross method developed by Robert Mueller and Signe Echols in their book The Lovers' Tarot *(see Further Reading, page 184). Mueller and Echols refer to this spread as the Heartprint method, or Tarot for Two. This is explored on the next page.*

TAROT FOR TWO

Here is a simplified account of the basic Tarot for Two approach. What's different about this method is that two decks are used instead of one. Each partner deals his or her own deck. To distinguish one pack of cards from the other, cards of different size should be used. Each of the ten positions in the Celtic Cross format then has two cards associated with it, as shown in the following diagram.

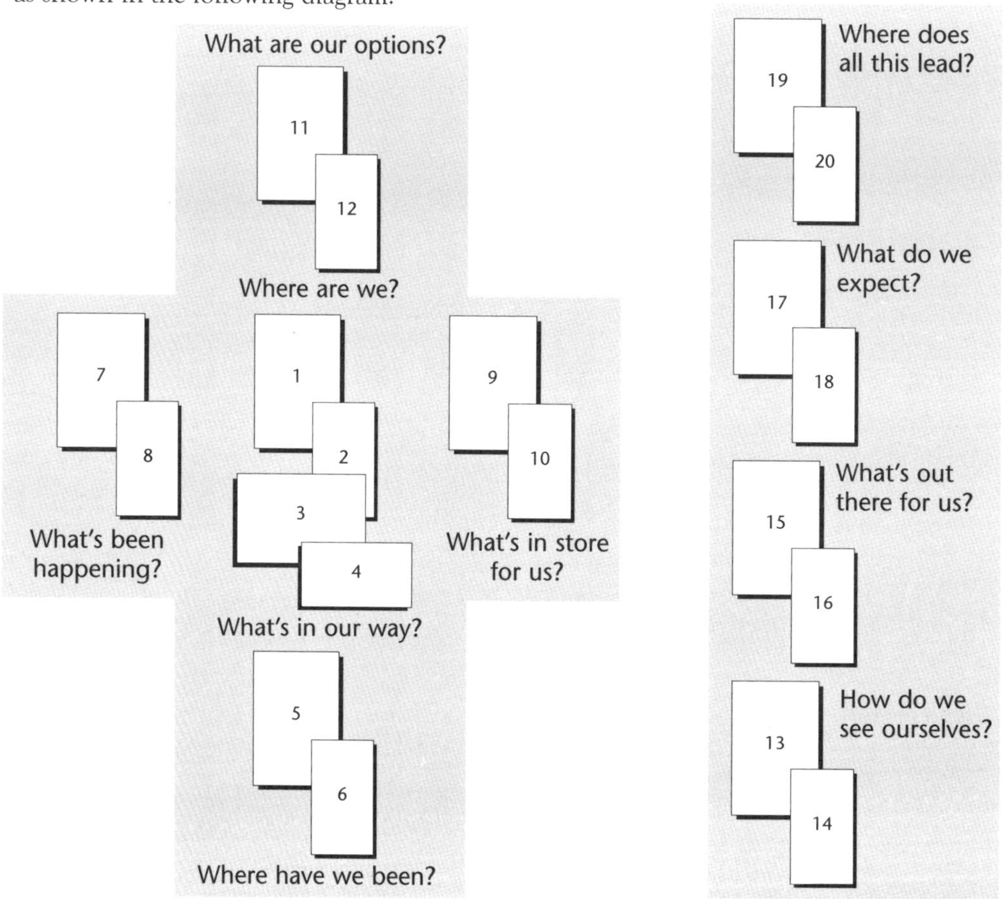

READING THE CARDS

For a joint reading, each of you will have agreed beforehand on the question to be asked. Each of you should now shuffle the cards in your own deck while focusing on the question for the reading. Focus on the question again as you deal out your cards alternately and lay them in position. Because you are asking a question jointly, you are both taking the role of the seeker. The reading should be structured as follows.

1. **Cards 1 and 2** refer to your present position, and reflect the influences relating to the question that you have asked. Both of these cards are, of course, the Significators. The essential joint message of Cards 1 and 2 is: "*Where are we?*" If you both chose the Lovers as your Significator, you are really asking: "*How is our relationship going right now?*"

2. Dealing alternately, take the top card from your own pack and place it sideways and faceup just below the two Significators (see opposite diagram). This is your crossing card, and you need to remember that the top of the card's design should face to the left. **Cards 3 and 4** now jointly represent the "immediate influences" affecting your present circumstances, and their essential joint message is: "*What's in our way?*" As mentioned before, some Tarot readers believe that the microcross of the cards laid so far (in this case, Cards 1 through 4) provides the essence of the reading, with the other cards in the spread spelling out the response in further detail.

3. **Cards 5 and 6** are placed vertically, directly below Cards 3 and 4. They jointly represent your distant past, and refer to the actual basis of your current concerns or the particular issues at hand. The essential message of Cards 5 and 6 is: "*Where have we been?*"

4. **Cards 7 and 8** are placed to the left of Cards 1 to 4. They represent your recent past, and reflect recent influences or experiences. The essential message of Cards 7 and 8 is: "*What's been happening to us?*"

5. **Cards 9 and 10** are placed to the right of Cards 1 to 4, and represent your near future. They refer to something that may happen soon. The essential message of Cards 9 and 10 is: "*What's in store for us?*"

6. **Cards 11 and 12** are placed directly above Card 1 and represent the outcome of the cross. They refer to events that will affect you in the future, and could include such things as meetings with other people, possible outcomes, influences, and choices. The essential message of Cards 11 and 12 is: "*What are our options?*" Once Cards 11 and 12 have been laid in this joint Tarot for Two layout, the basic cross is complete. The remaining cards are laid out in a vertical format to the right of the cross, and are known collectively as the staff.

7. **Cards 13 and 14** are the first cards in the vertical formation, and they are placed in the lowest position on the staff (see diagram on page 164). These cards identify how you both see yourselves, and will reflect your current concerns—such as anxieties, fears, or worries—in relation to the question that has been asked. The essential message of Cards 13 and 14 is: "*How do we see ourselves?*"

8. **Cards 15 and 16** are placed in the second lowest position in the vertical formation (see diagram) and refer to what the environment offers. They will reflect the opinions and influences of family and friends with regard to the question that has been asked. The essential message of Cards 15 and 16 is: "*What's out there for us?*"

9. **Cards 17 and 18** are placed in the second highest position in the vertical formation (see diagram), and refer to your greatest hopes or fears in relation to the question that has been asked. The essential message of Cards 17 and 18 is: "*What can we expect?*"

10. Finally, **Cards 19 and 20** are placed at the head of the vertical formation (see diagram), and complete the staff. In this spread they represent the final outcome. The essential

message of Cards 19 and 20 is: "*Where does all this lead?*" In the context of your developing relationship, this will be a very significant response. Do remember, however, to consider the central themes present in your spread as a whole, and be especially mindful of the messages sent by the other cards as well—they are all a part of your Tarot for Two reading.

WORKBOOK EXERCISES

1. Try the Three Aces method to answer a question about your relationship.
2. Then pose the same question with your friend or lover when using the Tarot for Two method. Which approach proved more satisfactory?
3. Does it help having both of you actively involved in dealing and interpreting the cards, or does it seem better to be working separately?

CHAPTER NINE

TAROT MEDITATIONS AND VISUALIZATIONS

Using the Tarot for meditation and visualization: How do meditation and visualization differ? How can I use both processes to learn more about my own inner world through the Tarot? How can visualizations based on the Major Arcana lead me along the pathways of the Tree of Life?

We can use the Tarot for **meditation** and **creative visualization**. Many forms of Eastern meditation involve eliminating imagery from consciousness altogether, thereby removing the distractions provided by the visual and verbal chatter of the mind. Creative visualization, which has a rather different emphasis, is sometimes referred to as "active meditation." Rather than negating visual imagery, it involves summoning specific images into our immediate sphere of perception. The symbols of the Major Arcana are particularly suited to both types of meditation, as they are mythic and archetypal. The Major Arcana as a whole presents a profound sequence of images that takes us into the very depths of the soul. Used individually, the images of the Major Arcana form the basis of separate meditations. When they are used collectively, we can see them as an archetypal sequence mapped upon the Kabbalistic Tree of Life. They form the basis of creative visualizations known as "pathworkings."

PATHWORKINGS

An important aspect of creative visualization is the process of engaging with images that arise into consciousness as if they were real. This means evoking images into consciousness in such a way that they are both convincing and alive within our spectrum of awareness. The idea of creating a pathworking is to enable the imagery of each Tarot card to come alive in the mind's eye, and to use the card as a mythic doorway that leads to a specific region of the psyche.

DEVELOPING YOUR VISUAL PERCEPTION

Some people claim they are not especially gifted visually, and don't see pictorial images when they close their eyes and enter the inner world we associate with the imagination. However, unless we were born blind at birth, each one of us has the potential to create visual images—even though we may be out of practice at doing so. We need to hone and utilize our powers of visualization in much the same way as we need to exercise our physical limbs in order to stay fit and healthy.

LEARNING TO VISUALIZE

Here is a simple exercise to expand your ability to visualize.

- Sit in a comfortable position.
- Close your eyes and relax.
- Now focus your inner awareness on one of the following, switching your attention completely to your powers of visualization:
  - a golden sun
  - a silver crescent moon
  - a blue circle
  - a red triangle
  - a colorful bird flying through the air

Did you notice any bodily sensation as you focused on these images? Did these visual images provoke any associations? For example, in yoga meditation a silver moon is a symbol of water, a blue circle is a symbol of air, and a red triangle a symbol of fire.

What color was the bird? Was it an exotic, unfamiliar species, or a bird you have seen frequently in your garden? Did you pay attention to the rich colors of its feathers, or the colors of its eyes and beak? How close did you get to the bird in your mind's eye?

Now you have tried focusing on one of these images, try visualizing the others.

Record any impressions or visual associations in your journal.

VISUALIZING THE SYMBOLIC COLORS OF THE TREE OF LIFE

Symbolic colors are important aspects of both the Tarot and the Tree of Life. When you have mastered the skill of visualizing, you will be ready to move ahead and learn to visualize the symbolic colors associated with the Tree of Life and the corresponding spiritual energy centers in the human body.

Here is a table showing the symbolic colors associated with the different spiritual energy centers on the Tree of Life. These spiritual energy centers are similar to the chakras in the Eastern mystical tradition. They are often shown in Kabbalistic diagrams, superimposed upon the human body. In this context, the human body represents the so-called Body of God.

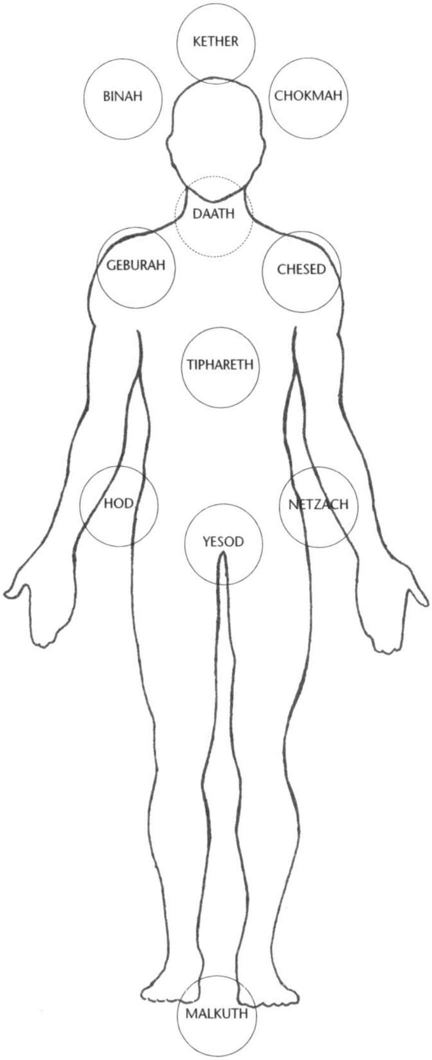

COLOR VISUALIZATIONS ON THE TREE OF LIFE

ENERGY CENTER	LOCATION	COLOR
Kether *The Crown*, or first point of Creation	Crown of the head	Pure white radiance
Chokmah Wisdom (the Father)	Left temple	Gray
Binah Understanding (the Mother)	Right temple	Black
Daath*	Throat	Mauve
Chesed Mercy	Left shoulder	Blue
Geburah Severity or Strength	Right shoulder	Scarlet red
Tiphareth Beauty or Harmony (the Son)	Heart	Golden yellow
Netzach Victory	Left hand	Emerald green
Hod Splendor	Right hand	Orange
Yesod The Foundation	Genitals	Violet or silver
Malkuth Kingdom or Earth (the Daughter)	Feet	Citrine, olive, russet, and black

** Known in the Kabbalah as the sphere of "Knowledge," Daath is sometimes referred to as the eleventh sephirah on the Tree of Life, although usually it is not shown. Daath represents the spiritual center on the central column of the Tree of Life that marks the crossover point between the first three sephiroth (the sacred energies of the Judaic Trinity, representing the unmanifest realm) and the seven lower spheres of manifestation (referred to in the book of Genesis as the Seven Days of Creation).*

VISUALIZATION: THE TREE OF LIFE AND THE HUMAN BODY

Take a few moments to relax, close your eyes, breathe in and out deeply, and visualize each of the energy centers in turn, commencing with Kether (representing Spirit) and concluding with Malkuth (representing everyday awareness in the world). Collectively, this process represents the descent of sacred power through the spiritual centers of the body.

As you do this, focus all your powers of awareness on the allocated color and also on its associated position on the human body. Developing your powers of visualization in this way will greatly assist you when it comes to exploring Tarot meditations and pathworkings, because pathworkings connect one energy center to another on the Tree of Life.

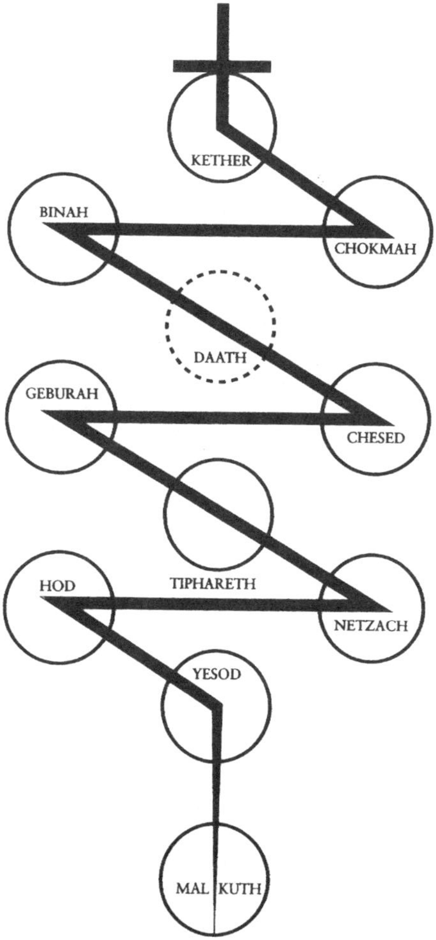

Drawing down the sacred energy from Kether to Malkuth

DEVELOPING SPIRITUAL AWARENESS

When we use the technique of creative visualization and apply it to the Tarot, we are effectively delving into the subconscious and spiritual levels of our mind. This involves engaging with those powerful images that the Swiss psychoanalyst Carl Jung called "archetypes"—personifications of universal sacred energies, such as the Sun God or the Lunar Goddess, which in all cultures and traditions have inspired religions, mythologies, and a rich variety of creative artistic expressions.

Irrespective of the spiritual path we are following in life, we should all learn to take responsibility for our own processes of personal growth. When we are using the Tarot to develop spiritual awareness, we should allow the archetypal images of the Tarot to speak to us in our own way. No interpretations of archetypal visionary images are ever fixed or immutable, and the interpretations of the cards of the Major Arcana are no exception. The key task here is to remain open to the messages conveyed to us through the archetypes as they communicate directly from the deepest and most profound recesses of our own beings.

TAROT VISUALIZATION ON THE STAR

The Star features the archetype of the Lunar Goddess. Relax, focus your powers of creative visualization, and ask a friend to read this text to you as you bring the imagery alive in your mind's eye:

In the night sky a golden star glows with crystal light. I see a beautiful naked woman standing in a fast-flowing stream. She is holding a flask aloft to the heavens and capturing life essence with this flask: life essence that flows down from the golden star above. Shimmering light flows through her body, and now she transforms into a translucent vessel herself, as she pours the waters of Life into a pool below. I watch as these waters overflow upon the surrounding earth. Everything around me now springs to life and offers new hope and possibility. The star maiden tells me that I, too, can become a vessel for the light, so that vitality and abundance can then flow through me in turn...And now the star maiden is leading me upon a path that takes me toward the golden star—the golden star that illuminates the heavens high above the earth...

THE MYTHIC PATHWAYS OF THE TAROT

When we visualize the Major Arcana as pathways on the Tree of Life, the sequence requires that we work our way back from the tenth and final sphere—Malkuth, which represents everyday awareness in the world—toward the mystical source of all Creation, represented by Kether. Having said that, it is also possible to undertake specific journeys on pathways located around the center or lower reaches of the Tree, or to meditate on specific Tarot paths by themselves. Here, once again, is a diagram showing the connections between the Tarot paths and the Tree of Life.

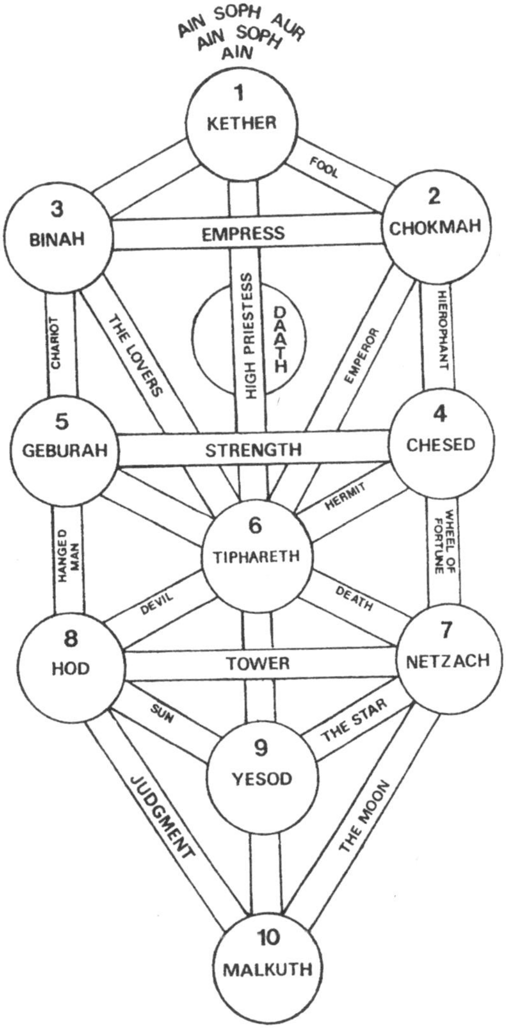

MEDITATION OR VISUALIZATION: AN EXAMPLE

Let us take a card from the Major Arcana, the World, as an example, to explain the different approaches of meditation and visualization.

We will first consider the simple meditation based on this card, provided in Chapter Four, page 87.

I embrace the World and give thanks for my life here on Earth.
I honor the Sacred Maiden whose dance is the Dance of Life.
I seek my life's true spiritual purpose.

This simple meditation has very little visual content, and allows the meditator to focus on some of the key themes attributed to this path:

- The idea of the Dance of Life, which represents the flux and flow of everyday awareness
- The idea that we are all on some sort of spiritual journey or quest, and are therefore seeking our personal spiritual purpose in the world

If we wanted to increase the visual content of this meditation and turn it into a visualization, we could expand it into something like the visualization on the following page.

VISUALIZATION TEXT FOR THE WORLD

Tides of energy flow all around me as I find myself in the presence of the Sacred Maiden of the Earth. Her pure face is filled with sunlight—light that nourishes the leaves and flowers in the deep, abundant valley—and her flowing hair is the color of golden wheat.

The Sacred Maiden dances naked upon the grass and a soft light plays upon her fair skin. Through her every movement I feel a sense of enrichment and warmth, and her radiant hair glistens like the newly risen sun casting its light across the fields.

In her eyes I see reflections of the Moon, and the Sacred Maiden tells me she will now lead me into the twilight world beneath the earth and beyond the sky, where she also rules the land of shadows...

And so now the Sacred Maiden prepares to take me on the first path of my sacred journey. She leads me through a passage in the earth toward a world beyond time...

Clearly these two texts—the first intended for simple meditation, the second for visualization—have very different impacts. One style may appeal to you more than the other, and this is largely a matter of personal taste. However, a couple of points need to be made here:

1. In the meditation version, the text is minimal, it is easy to remember, and it is very open-ended, allowing the imagination to head off in a number of different directions.
2. The visualization version, in contrast, is longer and more detailed. It is also more specific, referring to related mythological themes—in this case, to the Greek goddess Persephone, who was an Earth goddess and Queen of the Underworld (which symbolizes the gateway to the subconscious mind). This text would also be harder to commit to memory, and you would probably need to ask a friend to read it aloud to you as you relaxed, focused your awareness on the imagery, and then undertook the visual journey in your imagination.

CHOOSING BETWEEN MEDITATION AND PATHWORKINGS

As mentioned earlier, if you would like to focus on Tarot meditation, commit to memory the simple meditations presented in Chapter Four or prepare your own versions. If you would prefer instead to develop your powers of visualization, write your own pathworking texts and ask a friend to read them aloud to you as you visualize yourself undertaking each journey. Remember to write your texts in the present tense so they retain a sense of immediacy.

How you choose to prepare material for Tarot pathworkings is, of course, very much a matter of individual choice. The important thing is that each pathway should have the potential to come alive in your mind's eye as you venture forth on the inner journey. If you do opt to write your own visualization texts, it is a good idea to keep them slightly open-ended, to keep receptivity high and to convey the sense that there are mysteries that will be unfolded as you move through the process, so that one path can merge into another on the Tree of Life. By keeping the style of your pathworking open-ended, you also leave open the possibility that the gods and goddesses of the Tree of Life will share their wisdom and knowledge with you.

ANOTHER HINT FOR PATHWORKINGS

When you are practicing your pathworkings, you might find it helpful to begin by visualizing the sphere on the Tree of Life where your path actually begins, and end the session by visualizing your Tarot path merging into the sphere that is the final symbolic destination on the Tree. In each case you should visualize a sphere of radiant light, and the appropriate color can be identified by referring to the colors listed in the table of spiritual centers provided earlier. So, for example:

The World commences in Malkuth (visualize the path emerging from a combination of citrine, olive, and russet interspersed with black—these are the symbolic colors of Earth) and leads to Yesod (visualize the path dissolving into silver or violet radiance).

Tarot pathworkings become easier and more effective with practice. Although they are only a tool and not an end in themselves, they are endlessly fascinating, and you will find that they help to stimulate your imagination.

USING YOUR JOURNAL

Whether you have opted for the visualization or meditation approach, it is always useful to record your thoughts and impressions in your Tarot journal immediately after your inner journey, so that you can reflect on the different inspirational milestones that have begun to shape your spiritual path.

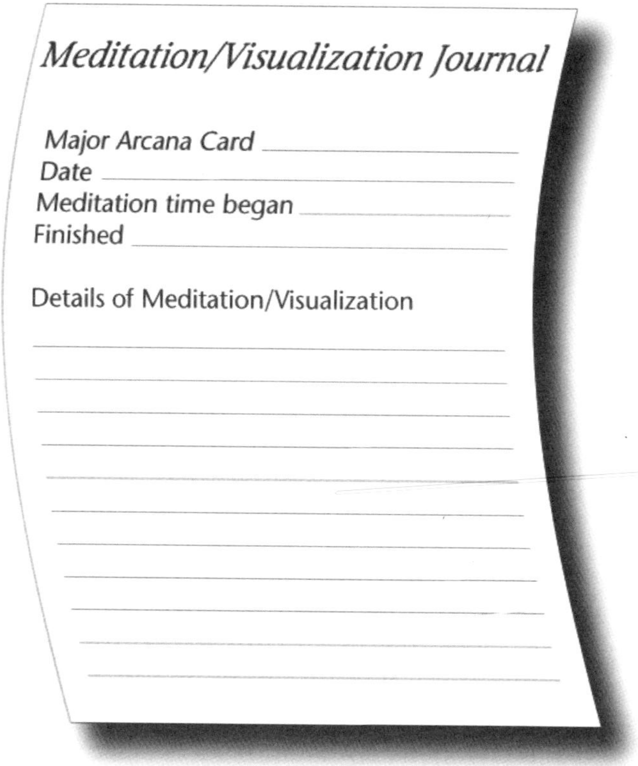

Remember to record your visualizations in your journal.

WORKBOOK EXERCISES

1. Colors have symbolic associations. What colors do you associate with the following sensations or feelings: pain, anger, enthusiasm, depression, happiness, and peace.
2. Try the simple meditation for the World, provided on page 175. Once you have relaxed, speak the words quietly to yourself. Don't hurry with this. Dwell on each sentence, focusing completely on the words and their meaning, and relating them to your life experience. Later, record any impressions or insights in your Tarot journal.
3. Now ask a friend to read aloud the text provided on page 176, while you relax and focus on the imagery of the Tarot card as it arises in your mind's eye. Evoke the presence of the Sacred Maiden of the Earth. What color is her hair, what color are her eyes? How does she present herself before you? Notice the soft light shining on her cheek. Sense the richness and fertility of the grain crops associated with this goddess. You may also wish to ask her a question—not aloud but through the power of thought. Remember what she tells you, because it could be a special revelation. When you feel the visualization is complete, bid farewell to the goddess and offer thanks for what you have received. Record all these impressions in your journal.
4. Having tried both the simple meditation and also the longer pathworking visualization, you may have a feeling about which approach works best for you. If you would like to explore pathworkings in more detail, go through all of the Major Arcana cards and prepare visualization texts for each one. This is quite a major undertaking and it will take you some time. Don't hurry the process, though. It is important to create a word sequence that will bring each card alive as you focus on it. Remember the following:
   - Make your descriptions poetic and visual so they stimulate your imagination.
   - Keep them in the present tense.
   - Ask your friend to read your pathworking texts to you at a pace that matches your powers of visualization. This may require a little practice.
   - Record all impressions from pathworkings in your journal immediately afterward. Otherwise, like dreams, precious details and impressions may be lost.

CHAPTER TEN

THE RESPONSIBLE TAROT READER

Becoming a responsible Tarot reader or counselor: How do I communicate with my client? How do I distinguish between fate and karma? How do I help others find their own solutions?

If after studying and exploring the Tarot in depth, you feel you would like to practice as a Tarot reader or psychic counselor, there are some important points to consider:

- It is vital for you to retain your own sense of professional and spiritual integrity.
- You need to adopt a strong ethical code of practice.
- Like many other Tarot readers, you could consciously seek some form of higher spiritual guidance—whether through prayer or through positive affirmations—so you do not unintentionally misguide the client through your interpretation of the spread.
- You need to express yourself clearly and speak to your client—the seeker—in a manner that he or she can relate to.
- As a reader you must communicate honestly and clearly what the cards seem to be saying even when there is an unmistakably negative feel to the energy of the spread—without threatening the seeker or making the seeker feel there is no possibility of escape.
- You need to explain to the seeker that Tarot cards indicate likely outcomes rather than fixed events, and there is always a possibility that a course of action can be modified. Even if the spread has negative connotations, there are still other options available.
- Avoid being dogmatic when you give a reading. If the seeker who has come to you is to some extent dependent on the direction of your reading, as some spiritual seekers undoubtedly are, a capacity for clear and effective communication—coupled with a genuine sense of optimism—will be important.

PERSONAL CONDUCT

Some Tarot readers may seek to project a certain mystique during their readings, perhaps with the intention of creating the impression that they have a psychic disposition or occult powers. Bear in mind, however, that what the reader is doing during a Tarot reading is using his or her intuitive skills to help the seeker draw on his or her own reserves of psychic and spiritual guidance. In short, the solution is within the seeker; the real answers to life's dilemmas come from within.

Using symbolic card configurations, the Tarot allows the Tarot reader's source of inner guidance to emerge. In this role the Tarot reader is a facilitator or guide, enabling seekers to find solutions that have previously eluded them. The reader is not the ultimate source of the solution itself. Humility is therefore an important quality in any Tarot reader. And it goes without saying that confidences shared during a Tarot session—that is to say, between the seeker and the reader—should remain private and confidential. A seeker is invariably in a sensitive state of mind when requesting a reading, and this should never be exploited.

FEAR AND PERSONAL RESPONSIBILITY

Some people seek out Tarot readers because they want to avoid taking responsibility for their own decisions. Even though the answers to their personal dilemmas will eventually emerge through their own shuffling of the cards and through the interpretation of the reading, there are some individuals who believe that it is the Tarot reader alone who has all the answers. Such people will often be seeking very specific, perhaps almost dogmatic, answers to their questions and will expect the future outlined in the cards to manifest itself in very concrete terms. It is also highly likely that they will later blame the Tarot reader if things do not turn out exactly as expected! Such people are dominated by fear and self-doubt, and unfortunately are also sidestepping the important issue of taking responsibility for their own actions. This allows them to take the role of the victim of fate. However, Tarot divination is not about outcomes set in stone. It is important to explain to the seeker that we all have to assume responsibility for our own thoughts and actions. This is the universal Law of Karma—the law of cause and effect—and it applies to the Tarot just as it applies to everything else.

KARMA AND FREE WILL

The essential principle of karma is that positive thoughts and actions produce positive outcomes and in turn create good karma, whereas negative thoughts and actions result in negative outcomes and create bad karma. This law applies to every conscious thought and action that arises in our everyday lives. According to the karmic philosophy of life, we literally create our individual futures by weaving karmic outcomes from the threads of our individual thoughts and actions.

Many people equate karma with fate and maintain that, because our past thoughts and actions help to create our future, our future is therefore predestined. However, karma is not the same as fate or predestination. The concept of fate implies that we are bound by a power beyond ourselves that somehow restricts us, and ensures that we will experience specific life circumstances that have been set out for us beforehand. According to the Law of Karma, we all have the power to shape and build our own future, and we will reap the consequences of our actions—good or bad—at a future time. By exercising our free will, we always have the option to break free from the conditioning of the past and rewrite our future. Clearly, this means that our future is not mapped out for us, or predestined.

This makes it clear that the future is not fixed. No act of divination, whether through the Tarot, astrology, numerology, or any other means, can point to an outcome that is guaranteed to occur. The existence of free will means that we always have the option to modify the likely outcomes of our thoughts and actions, and thereby create a different future.

FATE AND DESTINY

Although it is incorrect to equate karma and fate, it makes sense to link karma and destiny. Fate and destiny are not the same thing—fate is fixed, whereas destiny is changeable. It is our individual and collective destiny as human beings—through our acts of individual free will—to create different outcomes through our personal thoughts and actions.

Selfish thoughts and actions create a personal destiny based on the outcomes of these negative intentions, while virtuous actions create positive outcomes and a positive destiny. In this way the Law of Karma helps us to learn from the lessons of life itself.

Tarot readings reveal the forces driving our destiny. These forces are of our own making and will result in likely outcomes. They are not, however, supernatural forces, external to us, which somehow descend upon us and determine our fate. To this extent, the Tarot is not about predicting the future so much as about exploring the likely consequences of our individual thoughts and actions. We are all masters of our own destiny, and the Tarot is a wonderful guide that can help us balance body, mind, and spirit in the everyday world.

WORKBOOK EXERCISES

1. Try out a little karma exercise of your own. Think of something unfortunate that has happened to you recently. Try to pinpoint its immediate cause. Now look back beyond that cause to earlier factors that may have influenced this situation. How far back can you go in focusing on specific factors that contributed to this negative outcome?
2. Now think of something really good that has just happened to you. Explore the sequence of events that led up to this happy outcome. Try to get a real sense of the cause-and-effect impact of your everyday thoughts and actions. Do you believe now that you can create your own good (or bad) karma?
3. Reflect for a moment on the special qualities of the Tarot as a whole—the remarkable sequence of sacred images and their mythological associations, the themes of personal development and transformation, the blessings of guidance…Take time out to think of the Tarot cards as your special friend and mentor: a guide who is always there to assist your powers of intuition and deep, inner knowing.

FURTHER READING

Arrien, Angeles, *The Tarot Handbook*, Arcus Publishing, Sonoma, California, 1987.
Bonner, John, *Qabalah*, Skoob Books Publishing, London, 1995.
Case, Paul Foster, *The Book of Tokens: Tarot Meditations*, Builders of the Adytum, Los Angeles, 1989 (revised edition with color plates).
Case, Paul Foster, *The Tarot: A Key to the Wisdom of the Ages*, Macoy Publishing Co., New York, 1947 (reprinted, various editions).
Cavendish, Richard, *The Tarot*, Michael Joseph, London, 1975.
Connolly, Eileen, *Tarot: The Complete Handbook for the Apprentice*, Thorsons, London, 1995.
Crowley, Aleister, with Harris, Frieda (artist executant), *The Book of Thoth*, Weiser, New York, 1969 (first published 1944).
Fortune, Dion, *The Mystical Qabalah*, Benn, London, 1972 (first published 1935, reprinted various editions).
Gad, Irene, *Tarot and Individuation*, Nicolas-Hays Inc., York Beach, Maine, 1994.
Gray, Eden, *Mastering the Tarot*, Crown, New York, 1971.
Greer, Mary K., *Women of the Golden Dawn*, Park Street Press, Rochester, Vermont, 1995.
Kaplan, Stuart R., *Tarot Classic*, Grosset & Dunlap, New York, 1972.
Levi, Eliphas, *Transcendental Magic: Its Doctrine and Ritual*, Redway, London, 1896 (republished by Weiser).
Mueller, Robert, and Echols, Signe E., with Thomson, Sandra A., *The Lovers' Tarot*, Avon Books, New York, 1993.
Neville, E. W., *Tarot for Lovers*, Whitford Press, West Chester, Pennsylvania, 1987.
Papus, *The Tarot of the Bohemians*, Wilshire, Beverley Hills, California 1972 (first published in English 1892).
Pollack, Rachel, *Seventy-eight Degrees of Wisdom: Part 2—The Minor Arcana*, Aquarian Press, Wellingborough, England, 1983.
Pollack, Rachel, *Seventy-eight Degrees of Wisdom: Part 1—The Major Arcana*, Aquarian Press, Wellingborough, England, 1980.
Sharman-Burke, Juliet, *The Mythic Tarot Workbook*, Simon & Schuster, New York, 1988.
Summers, Catherine, and Vayne, Julian, *Self Development with the Tarot*, Foulsham, London, 1992.
Waite, Arthur Edward, *The Pictorial Key to the Tarot*, Weiser, York Beach, Maine, 1986 (first published 1910).
Wang, Robert, *The Qabalistic Tarot*, Weiser, York Beach, Maine, 1983.
Wanless, James, *Voyager Tarot*, Merrill-West Publishing, Carmel, California, 1980.
Ziegler, Gerd, *Tarot: Mirror of Your Relationships*, Urania Verlags, Neuhausen, Switzerland, 1989 (English language edition).

ACKNOWLEDGMENTS

Grateful acknowledgment is given to the following individuals and publishers for permission to reproduce pictures from their Tarot decks.

• Illustrations from the Rider-Waite Tarot, Golden Dawn, Aquarian Tarot, Tarot of the Witches, Tarot of Marseilles, Medieval Scapini, and Native American Tarot decks reproduced by permission of U.S. Games Systems, Inc., Stamford, CT 06902 U.S.A. © 1971, 1982, 1993, 1974, 1996, 1985, and 1983 respectively by U.S. Games Systems. Tarot of Marseilles is reproduced by permission of U.S. Games Systems/Carta Mundi, NV. Further reproduction prohibited. The Rider-Waite Tarot Deck is a registered trademark of U.S. Games Systems, Inc.

• Illustrations from the Motherpeace Tarot deck reproduced by permission, © 1981 Motherpeace: A pseudonym for Vicki Noble and Karen Vogel.

• Illustrations from the Aleister Crowley Thoth Tarot deck reproduced by permission of Aleister Crowley Thoth cards, © Ordo Templi Orientis, 1947, 2003. All rights reserved.

• Illustrations from the Egipcios Kier Tarot reproduced by permission of the publishers Editorial Kier S.A., www.kier.com.au.

• Illustrations from the Mythic Tarot cards are © Tricia Newell and are from the Mythic Tarot by Juliet Sharman-Burke and Liz Greene, published in Australasia by Simon & Schuster (1989) and reproduced by permission of Eddison Sadd Editions, London.

GLOSSARY

Ain Soph Aur (En Sof): In the Kabbalah, the sacred source of Creation—Ultimate Reality. Ain Soph Aur is beyond definition and has no symbolic correlations.

Celtic Cross: One of the best-known Tarot spreads, featuring ten cards in a cross and staff format.

Co-reading: A situation where two people both participate in a Tarot reading. The Celtic Cross spread is usually used (see Chapter Eight).

Court cards: There are sixteen Court cards in each Tarot deck and they are part of the Minor Arcana. In each suit (i.e., Wands, Cups, Swords, Pentacles) there is a King, Queen, Knight, and Page. The latter correspond to the elements Air, Water, Fire, and Earth, respectively.

Crossing card: The card placed horizontally across the Significator in the Celtic Cross Spread. It signifies "What's in my way?"

Destiny: The outcomes created by individual thoughts and actions (compare with Fate). Destiny is sometimes associated with the Law of Karma.

Divination: Methods used to identify likely future outcomes. Tarot cards are often used in divination to interpret personal destiny.

Elements: There are four elements—Fire, Water, Air, and Earth—and these correspond to the Tarot suits as follows: Fire (Wands), Water (Cups), Air (Swords), and Earth (Pentacles).

Fate: The principle that one's future is predestined and unchangeable (compare with Destiny).

Gypsy Spread: A forty-two-card Tarot spread in which the cards are laid out in six rows (see Chapter Six).

Hermetic Order of the Golden Dawn: A ceremonial magic group established in England in 1888 and has influenced the modern occult revival. Arthur Edward Waite and Pamela Colman Smith (creators of the Rider-Waite Tarot deck) were both members.

Kabbalah: The sacred tradition of Jewish mysticism, focusing on the Tree of Life. The word "Kabbalah" means "from mouth to ear," suggesting a secret oral tradition.

Karma, Law of: In Eastern mysticism, the principle that individual thoughts and actions create specific outcomes. Positive thoughts and actions result in positive karma and negative thoughts and actions result in negative karma.

Major Arcana: The twenty-two mythic cards of the Tarot deck, e.g., the Fool, the Magician.

Minor Arcana: The fifty-six suit cards of the Tarot deck. There are four suits: Cups, Wands, Swords, and Pentacles. Each suit contains the cards Ace to Ten, plus four Court cards (King, Queen, Knight, Page).

Pathworkings: Tarot visualizations using the Major Arcana. They are intended as meditative pathways linking the spheres of consciousness on the Tree of Life.

Reader: The person giving the Tarot reading.

Reverse meaning: The interpretation applied in a Tarot reading when a card is inverted during the dealing process.

Rider-Waite deck: The Tarot deck designed by Pamela Colman Smith and Arthur Edward Waite—first published by Rider in London in 1910 and still the most popular deck.

Ruler: The astrological planet or sign associated with a card in the Major Arcana (e.g., Saturn is the ruling planet for the World and Libra is the ruling sign for Justice).

Seeker: The person for whom a Tarot reading is given.

Sephirah (plural sephiroth): In the Kabbalah, an emanation or sphere of consciousness on the Tree of Life.

Seven Card Spread: A Tarot card spread utilizing thirty-three cards. The first seven cards dealt after shuffling are laid out as an indication of past, present, and future influences (see Chapter Seven).

Significator: A card representing the person for whom a Tarot reading is given (i.e., the seeker). In the Celtic Cross Spread, the Significator is a suitable Court card (see Chapter Three for guidelines), and in the Gypsy Spread the Significator is either the Magician or the Emperor for a male seeker and either the High Priestess or the Empress for a female seeker.

Staff: Cards 7 to 10 of the Celtic Cross Spread (numbering from bottom to top).

Suits: In the Tarot, there are four suits and these are associated with the four elements: Cups (Water), Wands (Fire), Swords (Air), and Pentacles (Earth).

Tarot journal: A personal journal used to record the results of Tarot visualizations and meditations.

Three Aces Spread: A Tarot spread utilizing three Aces—an ideal method for a quick "yes" or "no" from the cards.

Tree of Life: In the Kabbalah, the central diagram that symbolizes the way in which the sacred life force manifests in Creation. There are ten spheres of consciousness on the Tree of Life (Kether, Chokmah, Binah, Chesed, Geburah, Tiphareth, Netzach, Hod, Yesod, and Malkuth). The cards of the Major Arcana connect these spheres.

Yod: The first Hebrew letter in the sacred name of God: JHVH. Yods are found on several Tarot cards.

INDEX

MAJOR ARCANA

Page 44

Page 46

Page 48

Page 50

Page 52

Page 54

Page 56

Page 58

Page 60

Page 62

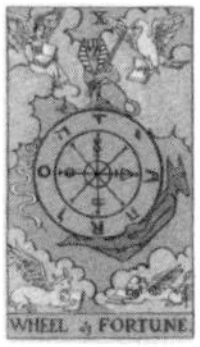

Page 64

Page 66

Page 68

Page 70

Page 72

Page 74

Page 76

Page 78

Page 80

Page 82

Page 84

Page 86

MINOR ARCANA

Wands
Pages 88–101

Cups
Pages 102–115

Swords
Pages 116–129

Pentacles
Pages 130–143